AN AMERICAN STORY

IN RED, WHITE AND BLUE

DEMPSEY J. TRAVIS

Urban Research Press, Inc.

www.urbanresearchpress.com

Copyright© 2002 Urban Research Press, Inc.
840 East 87th Street, Chicago, Illinois 60619 USA
Printed in the United States of America
First Edition
ISBN 0-941484-33-5

Library of Congress Cataloging-in-Publication Data.

Dedicated To:

Those among us who believe that the Constitution of the United States Of America and all of its Amendments are alive and well.

Acknowledgements

A good coach never changes the front line of a winning team. Therefore, with great pride, I salute the following players: Moselynne Travis, *my wife and motivator*, Ruby Davis, *senior researcher*, Pat Scott, *layout designer*, Stanley Moore, Regional Director U.S. Census Bureau, Jewell Diemer, Jasmine Dunning, a student trainee from the University of Illinois at Chicago and the Vivian G. Harsh Research Department of the Carter G. Woodson Regional Public Library.

Table of Contents

Part One:

Retrospective

...The early pioneers found that Indians in the Southeast had developed on this shore a high civilization with safeguards for ensuring the peace. A northern extension of that civilization, through the League of the Iroquois Indians, inspired Benjamin Franklin to copy their ideas when he drafted the federation of States...

...It seems a basic requirement to learn more about the history of our Indian people and others who contributed to making America a world class country. Americans generally have much to learn about the heritage of our Red and Black brothers. Only through serious study can we as a nation do what must be done if our treatment of Black and Indian people is not to be marked down on the calendar of time as a national disgrace...

John F. Kennedy
President of the
United States 1963

*Edited By: D.J. Travis
2002

Introduction
By: Dr. Carl Bell, M.D., F. A. C. Psych.

Dempsey Travis' story-telling skills have been well honed over a period of eighty-two years. His stories always elevate and promote African-American centeredness and self-esteem. At a deeper level, they offer grist for the African-American psychiatric mill as they illustrate how race and ethnicity effect mental functioning and personality. I have always found important, pithy information within the pages of his work that I never knew before reading many of his works. This book is no exception.

The first chapter describes various conflicts between newly settled European Americans and the Native Americans who were the first to live within the U.S. borders. African-Americans who understand how poorly Euro-Americans treated Native Americans, will take some comfort in learning how the new squatters took an initial beating from the red man. In this chapter, Mr. Travis also supplies the reader with some great census information about the number of Black freedmen and slaves in the United States in 1790. The classic photos of famous Native Americans are a real plus in that the reader can read the character on their faces.

Chapter two gives us some insight into President Thomas Jefferson's penchant for "brown sugar" that came in the voluminous frame of a female slave who answered to the name of Sally Hemings. Suprisingly, in this chapter we learn that, to make up for the "long course of injuries that had been committed on the African-American population," President Jefferson made plans for reparations that involved sending Black slaves back to the east coast of Africa.

Chapter three gives interesting facts about mulattos

and their presence in Chicago in the 1850s. In this chapter, Mr. Travis gives the reader some of his personal experiences of what he calls the "skin game battle" among Negroes. This chapter gives cause for reflection on why some African-Americans have been color-struck and employed the brown bag test as a tool to establish their social standing. This has been a long-standing struggle in the African-American community. The 1935 <u>American Council of Education (ACE) Studies of Negro Youth Personality Development</u> research projects developed by professors, Allison Davis, Ira Reid, E. Franklin Frazier, & Charles S. Johnson (African-American scholars in anthropology, sociology, and psychology at the University of Chicago) are perfect examples. This research project spawned <u>Color and Human Nature: Negro Personality Development in a Northern City</u> by W. Lloyd Warner, Buford H. Bunker, and Walter A. Adams published in 1941. It was distinguished by its controversial assessments of the effects of skin tones on African-American personality and social status. At the time of the study, the greatest status and prerogatives were associated with Blacks who were male, light skinned, and of upper class status. The effects of skin color especially fascinated the authors who commented that in the higher ranks of the Negro society a dark skin man will compete with white and light skin persons because the darker skinned man will sense their tendency to reject him due to his Negroid appearance. These scholars suggest such a man will need courage, ability, drive, and a disposition that will enable him to cope with the problems of making himself socially acceptable. Further, a northern born dark skin man expects greater opportunities and, more probably, has been led to regard instances of subordination of Negroes as 'prejudice' while a southern born dark skin man is aware of caste like restrictions at a much younger age and is more satisfied with his upper-middle class status. A southern born dark skin man was also felt to see the

V

achievement and maintenance of his upper-middle class status as a solid and gratifying achievement. Regarding light skin females, the authors remark that a light skin young woman who "has what it takes" in the way of education, nimble wits, and good manners, has a better chance than a darker young woman to climb socially, especially through marriage.

The authors observe that what a Negro has to say about his color and that of other people, together with his response to color evaluations, may often furnish a direct key to all or most of his thoughts about himself and his very existence. ACE (American Council of Education) studies found that seven factors predicted adjustment to racial status: 1) economic status, 2) patterns of social participation, 3) innate ability, 4) childhood experiences and child rearing practices, 5) health and emotional history and status, 6) birth order and status in the family, and 7) gender. These studies showed that these factors were associated with five patterns of adjustment to racial status: a) dodging caste-like barriers ("passing"), b) avoidance of contact with white groups ("complacency"), c) Black pride ("defending the race"), d) active or vicarious aggression ("striking back" at white affronts), and e) humility, clowning or resignation ("servility").

In chapter four, Mr. Travis' skills as an outstanding griot become manifest as he recounts a story of one of his contemporaries struggle with being light enough to pass. It is surprising to learn that many of the struggles we see in the 21st century were present in the mid 1950's. One would hope that more has changed in the last half century. In 1954, Gordon Allport wrote The Nature of Prejudice, in which he described how victims of prejudice respond. One response consists of an obsessive concern in which the insecurity about one's color causes extreme preoccupation with the problem and a haunting anxiety about what can happen. Another coping style is the denial of membership in the negative group while trying to assimilate into the wider culture, so darker skinned people may only associate with lighter people. Another defense characterized by withdrawal and passivity creates a mask of contentment for survival-a passive acquiescence of hiding the resentment allowing African-Americans to avoid the issue of color. Similar to the ACE studies, Allport also described clowning in which African-Americans make light of the problem, tell jokes about it, and try to minimize the impact of prejudice by using humor. Black Muslims exemplify another strategy. Their tactic calls for strengthening in-group ties due to the attack from the outside, thus developing clans of African-American folk. Since it is "OK" to cheat an outsider, African-Americans have also coped with prejudice by developing slyness and cunning.

Unfortunately, another style of living with prejudice involves identification with the dominant group causing self-hate. Sadly, this particular defense against prejudice caused the original division between dark and light-skinned African-Americans. Allport also describes some African-Americans who engage in aggression against one's own group and give examples of the class distinctions among African-Americans that remain very sharp, almost as though there were castes. Another unfortunate strategy against prejudice is to develop prejudice against out-groups. This strategy causes the establishment of a pecking order with higher status Blacks picking on lower status groups like new immigrants. Of course this method never worked as new immigrants do not accept their supposed lower status. Allport outlined another coping mechanism that involves sympathy with other members of an out-group. This strategy helps members of the prejudiced group to avoid developing a pecking order and prevents reactive prejudice against other out-groups. Some African-Americans choose militancy (fighting back) as a way to cope with prejudice. They refuse to be subjected to Euro-

American prejudice by seeking to get rightful territory and seriously striving to try to remove the stigma. Coping with prejudice can also cause African-Americans to make the error of striving for symbolic status, i.e., an off-center effort to gain status by showing wealth and achievement such as buying a car you cannot afford. In 1965, Dr. Kenneth Clark, the author of <u>Dark Ghetto</u>, referred to this phenomena as "overcompensatory grandiosity." Allport also positioned that with so much inner conflict, one wonders how much it translates into anxiety in African-Americans. Some scientists have suggested it is this anxiety that may be the source of the African-Americans' problems with hypertension. Finally, Allport suggested that some African-Americans respond to prejudice by developing a self-fulfilling prophecy, i.e., what people think of African-Americans to some extent determines what we become. So another negative reaction to prejudice is to meet the expectations of lower status.

In chapter five, we learn about a Black golfer's club-house that existed near Kankakee, Illinois in 1925. I wonder if Dempsey's wealth of information will ever run dry. I hope not. Someone among us must preserve and glorify our history so that our children can know who African-Americans are and how we have managed to survive with our dignity intact. After highlighting the white racism our medical and legal African-American giants faced, Mr. Travis takes a courageous step out on a very thin limb. He does so by raising the issue of "intra-black racism," one of Allport's coping strategies discussed above.

In chapter six the author shifts gears from ethno-graphic, storytelling into how the question of racial identity shapes the political reality for African-Americans in this country. While reading this section, I got a visual image of a Jaguar going from 4th gear into overdrive. Being one to turn a phrase Dempsey reminds us that Euro-Americans segregated "white and Black blood banks like coach cars on a train South of the Mason-Dixon line." For those nationalistic African-Americans who are faint of heart, like Allport, Mr. Travis also identifies the etiology of "intrablack racism" as stemming from "white racism." From reading this chapter, it becomes clear that "white racism" is a belief system that drives behavior and is as contagious as the common cold.

In chapter seven Dempsey describes the evolution of an African-American family from 1800 to 2002. This portion also recounts how some Euro-Americans "did the right thing" by their Negroes. It turns out that some slave owners benefited the Negroes they owned in their last wills and testaments. The journey of the Wheeler family is recounted and is quite fascinating as the family transitions from slaves to conductors in the Underground Railroad to African-American entrepreneurs. The chapter also highlights several historically Black colleges that have acted as a mainstay and anchor for African-Americans in the U.S.

In chapter eight, Dempsey Travis the Chicago African-American real-estate mogul and scholar takes on the relationship between African-Americans and Native Americans. Now there is a substantial huge profit in being identified as Native American, Dempsey addresses the recent increase in "Euro-Americans" who are claiming to be Native American. In this section of the book, Mr. Travis confirms an old saying in the African-American community "The only thing bigger than the white man's racism is his greed for money."

Chapter nine profiles the struggles of a Blackfeet Indian woman (Elouise Cobell) who is trying to secure financial justice for her people. It is amazing and disgraceful what this country has done and will do to cheat people out of their land and entitlements. This chapter goes into detail about how this little Native American woman successfully has taken on the USA political establishment and at this writing has won many victories.

Chapter ten informs the reader about a similar dastardly plot called the Teapot Dome scandal. This incident occurred in 1923, and involved another rip-off of Native Americans. The Teapot Dome disgrace is strangely similar to a story republished in an earlier book by Mr. Travis entitled <u>A Black Classic - The Negro Capitalist: A Study of Banking and Business Among American Negroes</u> by Abram L. Harris. In this case, the African-American rip-off involved an unscrupulous group of Euro-American business men who created the Freedman's Savings and Trust Company that swindled 61,131 recently freed African-American slaves out of $2,939,925.25 in 1874. The final chapter brings the reader up to date regarding the status of the most recent Federal rip-off that Elouise Cobell has been fighting. It only goes to show that many Euro-Americans continue to place themselves above the law, and how we all have to be careful lest we get trapped in a country that reverts to fascism. Of course should that occur, Dempsey Travis' books will be among the first to be burned as they herald the clarion call of freedom.

Carl C. Bell, M.D., F.A.P.A., C.C.H.P., F.A.C.Psych.
President and C.E.O.-Community Mental Health Council/Foundation, Inc.
Director of Public and Community Psychiatry; Clinical Professor of Psychiatry and Public Health, University of Illinois
Principle Investigator of Using CHAMP to Prevent Youth HIV Risk in a South African Township

Part One: An American Story

A Blackfeet medicine-pipe carrier wearing the
distinctive coiled hairdo of his station.

Chapter I

In The Beginning
The Founding Fathers
Caught Hell

When the nation's first census was taken in 1790 there were only two categories of people: "free whites" and "Black slaves". It literally took six hundred and fifty deputized federal marshals 18 months to take the census of 3.9 million American citizens excluding the Indians. The federal marshals spent the aforemention period of time banging on doors and bullying the occupants to give them access to their domicile. They went from house to house and shack to shack recording the names of the heads of the household and their children in addition to making margin notes of everything that moved within the homestead including the dogs and the cats.

However during the same period the Indians were literally delivering crushing blows to the Yankee land-grab-

3

President George Washington
1789 - 1796

Little Turtle
Chief of the Miami Confederacy

bers on the battlefield which was then our western frontier. The Yankee Doodle Dandies were soldiering under the direction of President George Washington's top General, Josiah Harmer. The general's soldier boys were being soundly beaten by Little Turtle, the very able Indian Warrior and Chief of the Miami Confederacy. The next defeat on President Washington's watch took place in 1791 under the command of the egotistical, grander than thou General Arthur St. Clair himself. Little Turtle was the field director in that battle which took place on the land that later became known as the borderline between the states of Ohio and Indiana. More than nine hundred of St. Clair's men were slaughtered and scores more wounded; and those that were still standing fled in panic to the hills. This battle marked the white men's second devastating defeat in their quest to expand the American western frontier

4

Chief Rain In The Face

Sitting Bull, Sioux Indian.
The best known of all Native Americans.

Chief Joseph of the Nez Perze.

Wolf Robe, Cheyenne

Colonel George Armstrong Custer

of the original thirteen colonies in the 18th century.

The most famous battle following the Civil War was Custer's Last Stand with the Indians in June 1876. That battle took place near the Little Big Horn River in South Dakota. Twenty-five hundred Sioux, Cheyenne and Arapahos Indians led by Chief Rain In the Face, Sitting Bull, Big Foot, and Chief Joseph rained down from the Dakota hills like man-eating red ants and wiped out Colonel George Armstrong Custer and all of his soldiers. The red men of the badlands did not even leave a dead tree standing.

Fourteen years later on December 29, 1890 a decade before the turn of the century the Great White Fathers thundered down with retaliatory revenge on the Indians as payback for the Custer Massacre. They shot down in cold blood little Indian children, women, and old men who could not defend themselves. They treated those people like wild animals when they opened fire on them at Wounded Knee Creek in the Badlands of South Dakota less than a day's horseback ride from the site where Custer made his last stand before dying of gunshot wounds with his boots on. Colonel George A. Forsyth led the charge with the late George A. Custer's famous Seventh Cavalry. In the white man's eyes free Indians and Negro slaves looked like red and black pepper in the same hot pot of boiling stew.

Thomas Jefferson, President George Washington and the other founding fathers were bonafide slave owners. In their first draft of what became the United States Constitution they designated that all Negro inhabitants male and female, be classified as three-fifths of a person for census purposes. The Negro population, including both the Black freedmen and the slaves numbered more than three-quarters of a million people. The abolitionist organizations estimated that approximately 14,000 of the Negroes in the populace were freed persons.

Jefferson justified his 3/5th of a man theory for

Negroes with the argument that "Blacks were inferior to whites in the endowment of their bodies and minds." That notion about Blacks was followed by additional racist propaganda that fostered the belief that Blacks were congenitally lazy, dishonest, and uncivilized (or uncivilizable.) Third, and of crucial importance in his major premise was the notion that all Blacks were sexually promiscuous and that Black men lusted after white women. The thought of interracial sexual intercourse involving Black men and white women haunted the early Americans' mind- set before and after the Civil War and only showing a little less intensity in the twenty- first century. However, a reverse thought pattern, occurred when white men and Black women were the main characters. The white masters literally had an open ended carte blanche credit card when it came to sexually exploiting their Black females. This open sexual beastiality applied to the general population thus was considered a non issue.

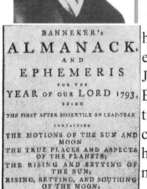

Benjamin Banneker

Benjamin Banneker, a freed Black who was an essayist, inventor, mathematical wizard and lay astronomer challenged Thomas Jefferson's theories about Black mentality by sending him a copy of his latest almanac which included his astronomical calculation as an example of Blacks' mental power. Jefferson responded by implying that Banneker was undoubtably an exceptional colored boy but one Black chap was not enough evidence for him to change his mind about the mentality of a whole race of people.

President Thomas Jefferson
1800 - 1808

Chapter II

Before We Were Colored

The social hierarchy among the Black slaves was determined by the work assignment allotted to them by the plantation owners. The house servants became the chosen ones and were considered privileged people in that they observed and took on the mannerisms of the lords and ladies of the manor. On the other hand the back-breaking sunrise to sundown cotton-picking field Negroes were spied upon by the stereotypical two-face snitching Uncle Toms and controlled by semi-illiterate, mean spirited, sunburned, horseback riding, bullwhipping, Simon Legree characters.

Interracial breeding between Black slave women and white men on this continent took on a life of its own when the lords of the big house decided that female household servants could serve in a sexual capacity in addition to washing, ironing, babysitting and cooking. The great white fathers' unamalgamated lifestyle with African women began in the original colonial states and territories in the seventeenth century and continued to escalate long before Thomas Jefferson, a widower and America's third president

Jefferson's Monticello Mansion in Albemarle County, Virginia.

and his longtime Black companion Sally Hemings, a mulatto slave girl took their sexual plunge. Jefferson was in bankruptcy when he died, hence, all of his slaves became the property of his creditors with the exception of Sally and their offsprings.

The Thomas Jefferson and Sally Hemings affair must have initially taken root when she was inadvertently selected to accompany Jefferson's youngest daughter Polly on a voyage to join her father in Paris, France in 1787. Sally resided in Europe for two years with Jefferson and his daughter. It has been said that she returned to Monticello with an infant son although the boy is not listed on Jefferson's chattel ledger. Sally bore for Jefferson at least

14

four children that he recognized and possibly as many as six. Jefferson's Farm Book lists the following as his off-springs with the exception of Sally. Sally was possibly Jefferson's father-in-law's daughter because she looked enough like his late wife to have been her youngest sister. Jefferson and Sally's children are listed as follows by their given names and birth year.

Beverly, 1798
Harriet, May 1801
Madison, January 1805
Eston, May 1808

DNA test performed in the 1990's on descendants of Thomas Jefferson's family and on the great-grandchildren of Jefferson's young slave Sally Hemings, offered positive proof that the third president of the United States was the father of her children. The allegation is based on blood samples collected by Eugene Foster, a retired pathologist in Charlottesville, Virginia.

Lander, a DNA expert at the Whithall Institute in Boston, said Foster's evidence showed there was a less than one percent chance that a person chosen at random would share the same set of Y chromosomes that exist in the Jefferson lineage.

The affair between Jefferson and Hemings was so well known that a popular ditty about their love life was written to the tune of Yankee Doodle Dandy:

Of all the damsels on the green,
On the mountain or in the valley,
A lass so luscious never seen as
Monticellian Sally,
Yankee Doodle whose the noodle?
What wife was half so handy?
To breed a flock of slaves for stock

A blackamoor's a dandy.

Among the newspapers that printed the ditty were: Richmond Examiner, Richmond Recorder, New York Evening Post and Boston Gazette.

In addition to President Thomas Jefferson's eyes for Black women he also had a reparation plan for the Black population generally. In one of his dispositions he said: *For those unfortunate people, there are two rational objects to be distinctly kept in view. Firstly, we must establish a colony for them on the east coast of Africa. ... By doing this, we must give them retribution for the long course of injuries we have been committing on their population... Then by degrees, send the whole of that population from among us, and establish them under our protection, as a separate, free and independent people... Any place on the coast of East Africa should answer this purpose...*

On the other hand, George Washington decreed in his will: *that his mulatto man William Lee be given his freedom immediately or given the option to stay in the situation that he was presently in. In any case I will give him an annuity of thirty dollars per year for the rest of his natural life. I also expressly forbad the sale or transportation out of the Commonwealth of Virginia any other slaves that I may possess under any circumstance.*

Thomas Jefferson

Portable writing desk upon which Thomas Jefferson wrote the first draft of the Declaration of Independence in Philadelphia in 1776.

President Abraham Lincoln
1861 - 1865

Chapter III

In The Days That Blacks Begin to Turn White

As a result of this ethnic mixing there was a mushroom of mulattos like Sally Hemings and octoroons who were an off-white shade in skin texture. Their offsprings constituted 37 percent of the freed Negro population. The majority of the Negro property owners in Chicago, Illinois during the first half of the 19th century were mulattos.

In the 1850 census report the government instituted some significant changes in revamping the form. The new budget included expenditure for training federal marshals in the scientific methods for collecting, documenting, and reporting census data. Moreover, the 1850 census forms marked the first time that detail occupational information and skin differentiation defined the complexion of Blacks. Note the following:

Free Negro Property Owners In Chicago - 1850

Ward	Name	Age	Property Location	Old Occupation	New Occupation	Value of Real Estate
2	James B. Bower	33	Dennis Lardon's	Hairdresser	Laborer	$1,600.00
2	John Jones	34	Lake Street	Tailor	Same	1,500.00
2	*Maria Smith	39	39th & Buffalo Street	not known	not known	1,000.00
3	A.J. Hall	28	North Wells Street near Harrison	Barber	Same	400.00
3	W. Wynder	30	183 West Monroe Street	Cooper	Cooper	500.00
4	C.C. Hansen	39	250 West Madison Street	Barber	Same	3,000.00
9	Henry Knight	30	126 Dearborn St.	Livery Stable	Same	10,000.00

Note: Included among colored property owners were persons of the following pigmentation:

African - 100% pure black
Mulatto - 50% black
Quadroon - 25% black
Octoroon - 12.5% black
Total number of property owners = 7
* She was a former slave master's kept woman
The first labeled mixed-race in the census was mulatto in 1850. By 1890, due to the insistence of an Alabama Congressman, the terms quadroon and octoroon were added to the National Census forms.

Source: 1850 U.S. Census Report, and City of
Chicago 1850 Directory
Graphics: Urban Research Press

The offsprings of American Blacks, whites and Indians were endowed with a rainbow of shades. There were

20

Blacks with a reddish hue as well as those who had a blue cast in their skin tone. Plus, there was another group of Blacks that had a beautiful deep chocolate brown complexion. Somewhere between the pure black and mulatto skin tone there were individuals who were beige, tan and teasing high brown. These various skin shades set the stage for an ongoing intra-color struggle for status that has lasted into the twenty-first century.

Originally the skin game battle was primarily between the master's light skin house Negroes and dark skin field Negroes. Keep in mind that many of the house Negroes were direct offsprings of the plantation masters. A classic example of the interactions between pure Black and some

mixed blood products may be seen in a movie entitled "Imitation of Life" (1934). The film was originally exhibited internationally in the mid nineteen thirties and it starred Fredi Washington, a former Cotton Club chorus girl and actress, Louise Beavers and Claudette Colbert. Fredi

Fredi Washington the dancer and actress was an octoroon.

Washington, an octoroon in real life was married to Lawrence Brown, a mulatto trombone player with Duke Ellington's Cotton Club "Jungle " Orchestra. Fredi had blue eyes and played the role of a Black girl passing for white and answering to the name of Peola. She passed for a WASP in the film, which is still a common practice in the Black community and known as "crossing over". In this movie, Louise Beavers played the role of Fredi's mother. She was a fat, dumpy dark skin woman who became famous playing the part of Aunt Delilah, Claudette Colbert's cook.

Louise Beavers played the role of Washington's mother in the movie "Imitation of Life" in 1935.

She created a popular, money making pancake formula while in the employment of Colbert. In spite of her financial success, Delilah was totally rejected by her pale skin daughter. When Beaver died Fredi did not show any remorse or emotion at her mother's funeral that is until the pallbearers began lifting her casket into the hearse.

White folks found the picture both sensational, comforting, and reassuring because it ended with the implication that any Black person who tried to pass for white would ultimately be stricken with some measure of grief at the end.

In 1935, during my high school years at DuSable High School in Chicago, there were Negro-Americans at my all Black secondary school who were very much involved in a bloodless war over skin color. In search of an image, a group of fair skinned Negro students formed a Peola Club at my high school in 1936 they had been influenced by "Imitation of Life". A Colored individual had to pass the brown bag test (that is your skin had to be lighter than a brown paper bag) before one would be considered for membership. This group was composed of mulatto girls who were longhaired, with pale skin, thin lips and natural green, blue, or hazel colored eyes. (This was decades before color lens inserts.)

During the Depression era, very few people (colored or white) could afford to have plastic surgery on their nose or braces for their teeth. However, in spite of these young ladies Anglo deficiencies and their poverty stricken circumstances these light skin girls were still considered a real catch by some wealthy professional dark skin males. They were the women of preference.

In 1935 Du Sable High School in Chicago, Illinois opened as the first brand new Secondary Public Institution to be built in the heart of the colored community.

Am I Black or White ?

Chapter IV

What Am I Black Or White?

America's skin disease affected the Brown family in a sundry of ways. My young friend, John London Brown's parents were light-skinned. His mother could pass for a White Anglo Saxon Protestant (WASP), and his father's skin tone was several shades darker than his wife's. If Dr. Johnny Brown, Sr., had chosen to affect a Hispanic or Portuguese accent, he could have easily been assimilated into the white world.

Johnny, who was blue-eyed and blond like his mother, never sensed that the world was different for him until he was 6 years old. Thus his rude awakening came in January 1945, near the end of World War II, when he entered the first grade at the A.O. Sexton Elementary School at 6020 S. Langley in the Washington Park subdivision on the south side of Chicago. When he returned home after his first day in school, his mother asked:

"What color is your teacher? Is she Colored or white?"

The Harris' are two first cousins who resided on Chicago's south side in the Woodlawn community shortly after the turn of the 20th century.

"What color are we?" Little Johnny queried.
His mother replied, *"We are colored."*
"The teacher is White," Johnny replied.

Several days later, Johnny's mother visited the Sexton School and discovered that the teacher was as Black as anthracite coal. The little boy's confusion was under-standable because he had observed that the teacher's skin color was the opposite of his mother's glistening white face and his own milky white hands. He logically concluded that since they were Colored, his teacher must be white.

In the spring of 1947, Johnny's father, who was a renowned social science professor at the University of Chicago, accepted a 4-month assignment to do a study in Hawaii. Throughout their ocean voyage, people asked Johnny and his brother Steve what nationality they were. By the second day at sea, the bombardment of questions about race caused Dr. Brown to erupt in anger. He advised his two young sons to tell anyone who asked them about their nationality to state that they were Americans.

One elderly lady became a pain in the behind by asking these boys several times a day, *"What race are you?"* On their fourth day at sea, the boys made up something they thought would be incredible enough to squelch her inquisitiveness. They told the woman that they were one-sixth Greek, two-sixths Indian, one-twelfth Irish, and every other combination they could think of. The lady did not bother them with her nationality nonsense for the rest of the voyage.

The young Brown brothers grew and matured so much as first graders that their parents enrolled them in the University of Chicago Laboratory School in the second grade. There were only a handful of Black kids in their class. There were five Blacks in a class that was one grade ahead of them. Most of the Black children were sons and daughters of professionals and many, like the Brown brothers, were so light-skinned that they could have passed for white. The brothers knew that 98 percent of the residents in their East Woodlawn neighborhood were Black, and the Hyde Park neighborhood was where most of the white students lived was just across Cottage Grove the eastern marginal line. Since their parents had friends among the Black and white races, and all of their father's colleagues at the university were white, the Brown children escaped the total impact of Jim Crow.

In sixth grade, Johnny was fairly popular among the children at the Lab School. He had lots of white friends, both male and female. At the beginning of the semester in seventh grade, he was invited to attend a dance at the home of a white classmate. That proved to be his last invitation to such an occasion. He later learned that no other Black children had ever been invited to parties given by their white classmates, and it took him a little while to get a fix on what had happened.

Although the Blacks at the Lab School were not invited to any parties, groups of white and Black students would go to the Hyde Park movie theater on Saturday afternoons. As the tree sap rose in the spring, the students began pairing off into couples. Johnny asked several white girls in the group to be his date, but they turned him down. He didn't understand because he was tall, blond, blue-eyed and handsome by WASP standards. Suddenly, a light went on in his head one afternoon when one of the white girls he was pursuing for a date said, *"You will have to talk to my mother."*

Johnny told his mother, who called the girl's mother only to be told that she didn't want her daughter going out with a Colored boy. It was a profound and sobering experience for Johnny Brown when confronted with the fact that although he was popular in the classroom, he could not socialize with the white students after dark. The realization hit him with a bluster more chilling than a -20° January wind in Chicago.

Johnny avoided being devoured by hate and anger by associating with a group of white non-athletic, not-too-bright classmates he called misfits. Today, some of them are counted among the avant garde in the professional and business community and are known for not allowing race to become a barrier to friendship. Several of his schoolmates have become leaders in Fortune 500 companies.

After completing eighth grade, Johnny transferred to

Hyde Park High School, where approximately 40 to 50 percent of the students were Black, 40 percent were Jewish and
about 5 percent were Japanese. Johnny and his friends
referred to Hyde Park as "Zebra Tech" because the students
embraced integrated socialization. The choir, the basketball
team, the football team and the parties were integrated.
White guys were going out with Black girls and Black guys

**Herbie Hancock, a former Miles Davis associ-
ate was a fellow student of the Browns at
Hyde Park High School.**

were going out with white girls. The socialization drove
their parents nuts. There was no way the Jewish parents
could stop their kids from going to Black parties.

Many of the friendships formed between the Browns and
whites at "Zebra Tech" have survived until this day. When
these old friends meet, their conversations are laced with
talk about the uniqueness of their years at Hyde Park High
between 1955 and 1959. They remember when Herbie

Hancock, the now-famous pianist/composer, and orchestra leader was elected King of Hyde Park High and thus he became the first Black to attain that lofty status. Hancock's election showed Johnny that there wasn't anything wrong with being Black, and that it was not his fault that he went from a popular person to a pariah at the University of Chicago Lab School. Almost immediately after transferring to Hyde Park High, just three blocks south of the Lab School, Johnny became a popular guy again.

Steve Brown left the Lab School a year after his brother Johnny because he encountered similar racial problems. He had become a reject and punching bag for some of the white toughs. When Steve arrived at Hyde Park High, he rediscovered his outgoing personality and ability to function as a top-flight student, thus mirroring his brother's overnight transformation.

Johnny didn't do too well academically at Hyde Park but he excelled in Popularity 101. For his senior year, his parents sent him to Kushon Academy in New England, an institution with a reputation for accepting a few Black students, with the purpose of preparing them for an east coast Ivy League education.

When Johnny walked into the boys' dorm at Kushon, the 17-year-old Chicagoan didn't know a soul. The dorm was jammed with students engrossed in watching a baseball game on television involving the Milwaukee Braves. It might have been the World Series.

The first words that Johnny heard were, *"Kill that coon!"* They were talking about Hank Aaron, who was up at bat. Johnny thought, *"Well, if they're gonna kill Hank Aaron on TV, they're gonna kill me now because I'm right at their fingertips."* He was terrified. He heard racial references that he had never heard before: like coon, jake, spade, and jungle bunny. *"Oh my God , what is going to happen to me?"* he sighed.

The presence of his first cousin, James, who was

lodged across the road in another dorm offered Johnny little comfort because they were the only two Black males in the school. Johnny was scared dungless, a reaction his mother anticipated that he would have in a new environment a thousand miles from home. She had suggested that he take pictures of the family to keep on his dresser for those occasions when someone would come in and ask, *"Well, who are these people?'* Johnny could respond, *"That's my family."*

"Hopefully," his mother said, *"They will get the message and you won't have to explain or wear a sign saying, 'I am a Negro.'"* That proved to be a very effective antidote for countering racial exclusivity.

Although he was at Kushon for just seven months, he was elected the most popular person in his class; his cousin James was the second-highest academic achiever in the school's history.

After graduating from Kushon Academy, Johnny went to Grinnell College, in Grinnell, Iowa, which he described as "a piece of cake" because he encountered few racial problems during the four-year tenure. The only glimpse of racism occurred when he was initially assigned to a room with two other Blacks. When his father heard about it, he hit the ceiling and called the president of the college. *"How could a progressive school put three Colored kids in the same room*?" Dr. Brown bellowed.

The boys were immediately switched to different quarters, but after spending one night with their new roommates, they decided they would rather room together. Thus, they became roomies, by choice, for the four years they were at Grinnell.

The college also attempted to match the three Black guys with three Black girls on the campus, but the guys paid the school's matchmaking efforts very little attention. They dated white as well as Black girls, causing Johnny to describe Grinnell as *"kind of an ideal world."*

31

**Cecil Partee,
Senate Leader and
States Attorney**

Law school proved to be a totally different environment from Johnny's Grinnell experience. He attended Northwestern Law School in Chicago, which he said, "Was filled with absolute bigots." There are only two people from his class that Johnny has maintained any communication with today.

Johnny recalls that when he enrolled at the law school, he filled out his application about race and religion honestly, and was assigned a single room at Abbott Hall on the downtown campus off Lake Shore Drive. He like Cecil Partee, R. Eugene Pincham and Harold Washington was the only Negro in his class at Northwestern Law School. Jewish students, were paired off with other Jews or given a single room.

Johnny describes the demographics of the Northwestern Law School student body as about one-third Chicago Jews and one-third WASP from all sections of the country.

Johnny recalls: *"They were really a bad group of people." He said "The law students were unlike any other students I had known, with their 'We don't like niggers' attitude. Moreover, during my three years at the law school, they never abandoned their dislike for Blacks. It was a tough place. A lot of the Irish guys were from the Gage Park area on the Southwest Side of Chicago. We're talking about the early '60s, when civil rights issues and*

Judge R. Eugene Pincham

Harold Washington, Chicago's first Black Mayor.

Dr. Martin Luther King, Jr. were in the forefront of the news."

After the end of his first year in law school, Johnny said *"I had swallowed as much of the bigotry as I could stomach without regurgitating green liver bile in the middle of the lecture hall. The situation was so unpleasant that I took every opportunity to leave Abbott Hall for the sanctuary of home with my parents, who had moved from East Woodlawn to Hyde Park."*

Johnny didn't fare very well academically at the law school because he could not concentrate on his studies in that racially charged environment. He told his father that if he didn't dropout, the school would put him out.

Dr. Brown asked, *"Don't you know any members of the faculty? Don't you know any students?"*

Johnny replied, *"I*

just can't stand it. Dad, you can't imagine how awful it is." It was a devastating confession for the young man who had been the most popular person in his senior class at the Kushon Academy and was elected class president twice at Grinnell College.

Johnny insisted that he was going to dropout, but his father stomped his foot down on the living room floor and screamed: *"There must be somebody that you can talk to."*

After some thought, Johnny remembered John Kaplan, his professor in a real estate law class. Kaplan was a mild-mannered man who had displayed a real sense of humor. In addition, Kaplan had written a report on desegregating New Rochelle, N.Y., for the Civil Rights Commission on Housing, and Johnny reasoned Kaplan's ethnicity and experience might have given him some empathy for another minority.

Brown was on the mark because Kaplan told Johnny that dropping out of law school would be a big mistake. *"I'm sure you've taken note of the idiots around here,"* he told Johnny. *"These are some of the dumbest people I've ever taught. There is no reason that you can't do the work better than they can. I know that you're smarter than nine-tenths of them, and I'm telling you to stay in school. I will see that the professors in each of your classes give you some attention."*

Johnny moved back into Abbott Hall on North Lake Shore Drive, Kaplan kept his promise and Johnny's grades improved dramatically.

In his last year in law school, Johnny Brown assembled a resume' that included his activities with the Black Law Students Alliance.

Johnny recalls his first interview with a major corporation in Detroit. *"I had already been interviewed by two officers of the firm, and things were going great. I felt that I had the job in the bag. A third member of the firm's interview team looked at my resume and came to a dead*

34

halt when he reached the section on student activities. He looked at Johnny and glanced back at the resume' several times before continuing the interview."

Brown recalls the following question and answer session:

"Johnny, what is the Black Law Students Alliance?" the corporate counselor asked.

"It's an organization of Black law students at my law school," Johnny replied.

"Well, I've got a couple of more questions for you," the interviewer said. "Number one, why do Blacks need an Alliance like this to begin with?"

"It's somewhat of a support group for each of us," Johnny retorted. "Our law school doesn't have a great number of minority students to begin with. The Black Law Students Alliance is kind of a social group and also kind of a close-knit support group."

"I don't understand why Blacks would need their own separate group," the lawyer said.

Johnny replied, "For many years Blacks have had to have their separate groups because they weren't allowed in majority groups. For example, for years the American Bar Association and the Chicago Bar Association did not permit any Blacks to become members."

Johnny had anticipated the next question. "Why are you in the group?" the corporate counselor asked.

"What do you mean why am I in that group?" Johnny

35

responded.

"I don't understand how you got in the group," the counselor snapped back.

"What do you mean you don't understand how I got in the group?" Johnny retorted.

"Did they have some special type of admissions policy or were you just simply voted in?" queried the corporate counselor.

Johnny decided that he was not going to let the man off the hook. "I decided I would make him ask me the gnawing question point-blank. Finally after a group of idiotic questions that you wouldn't expect from a lawyer in a major corporation, he finally asked me the $64,000 dollar question, 'Are you Black?'

"What difference does it make?" Johnny snapped. "Don't you know it's unlawful to ask about race? What is the purpose of that question?"

The counselor softly replied, "I'm just trying to figure out how you got into The Black Students Alliance."

Johnny decided he wasn't going to waste more time playing hide-and-seek on the race issue. "Yes, I am Black," Brown blurted out. "And that's why I'm a member of the organization."

The corporation counselor's face became cherry red. From that point, the interview went downhill.

Johnny said, "I knew when I prepared the resume that if I omitted putting in the fact that I was affiliated with the Black Law Students Alliance I could have gotten a number of jobs and passed myself off as a white boy. But I have elected not to live a lie."

Congressman Adam Clayton Powell Jr.
Democrat, N.Y. 1944-1970

Chapter V

Why Must I Be So Black and Blue?

Music By: Thomas " Fats" Waller, and lyrics by Harry Brooks and Andy Razaf

Cold, empty bed,
Springs hard as lead,
Pains in my head,
Feel like Old Ned,
What did I do
To be so black and blue?

No joy for me,
No company,
Even a mouse

Fats Waller, pianist extraordinare and composer.

Ran from my house;
All my life through,
I've been so black
and blue.

I'm white, inside;
It don't help my case;
'Cause I can't hide
What is on my face.

Oh! I'm so forlorn,
Life's just a thorn,
My heart is torn;
Why was I born?
What did I do
To be so black and
blue?

How sad I am,
Each day I feel
worse;
My mark of Ham
Seems to be a curse.
Oh! What did I do
To be so black and blue?

Congressman Adam Clayton Powell, D-N.Y., who was Black inside but white outside when he joined a white fraternity as a freshman student at Colgate University in Hamilton, New York in 1927. Prior to Powell's racial identity being discovered he was housed in the freshman dormitory with a white roommate, who upon learning that Adam was Black demanded that he move out of the room posthaste. For a period thereafter he was ostracized by both his Black and white classmates. He was not fish or fowl. This experience caused him to become one of the most audacious Black men in Harlem. He did not change his demeanor after being elected to Congress where he became the fourth Black man to sit in that august body in the twentieth century. After taking his seat in that chamber in January 1945, he expanded his reputation by becoming the most flamboyant Black political figure in America.

Herb Jeffries,
the singing bronze cowboy.

Herb Jeffries, a vocalist with Duke Ellington's famous Cotton Club Orchestra, had a milk white complexion like Powell. One night in September 1940, while a patron in a nightclub, he was sharing a table with some whites, including a drunk who stared at Herb and blurted, *"I assumed you were Colored based on your recordings. But you aren't. Are you?"*

"What do you mean by Colored?" Jeffries retorted.

"Why, anyone with Negro blood," the man replied.

"Is two drops enough to qualify?" inquired Jeffries.

The man nodded, "Yes."

"Negro blood must be some mighty powerful stuff," the singer recoiled. "If, for instance, you had a black paint so powerful that two drops of it would turn a bucket of white paint black that would undoubtedly be the most powerful paint in the world wouldn't it."

Jeffries was on target about the potency of black blood in the minds of white racists.

Some fifteen years later in the fall of 1955, there was a news wire service story that stated that Black fullback Bobby Grier would sweat, bleed and probably elicit cheers on a Dixie football field. The story upset the people of the sovereign state of Georgia and riled the sports circles around the world, the idea so clouded the mind of the then Governor, Marvin Griffin, that even his red neck henchmen begged him to "grow up."

Attorney Linda Chatman, graduate of the University of Chicago Law School.

Linda C. Chatman is a native Chicagoan and the proud possessor of an engraved Doctor of Juris Prudence Degree from the University of Chicago Law School. At the time I interviewed her on November 2, 1992 she had recently been questioned by a Sun-Times reporter about her reactions to being referred to as a "Black Bitch" during an employment interview at the Chicago office of the international law firm of Baker and McKenzie.

She described that particular interview as follows:

I was ushered into this canyon sized office and escorted down a long corridor from room to room where I was introduced and engaged in brief conversations with different partners and associates of the firm. The final interview was with an Attorney O'Caine one of the senior partners and a "rainmaker" for the firm. He initially asked me the usual stock questions based on the information he had gleaned from my resumé. He noted in my resumé that I was a golfer. The idea of my being a Black female golfer ignited a series of unusual questions. The first question out of his mouth was: 'Why don't Black people have their own country club?' I simply sat there and looked at him because I don't think he really expected an answer. He then rambled through my curriculum vita for another several seconds and raised his head to make eye contact and blurted: 'Jews have their own country club.' Then as an afterthought he mumbled: 'I guess there aren't too many golfers in the ghetto.'

(From 1925 until 1946 most of Chicago's elite Colored golfers belonged to a Negro owned country club called Sunset Hills, it was located next to the Kankakee River near Kankakee, Illinois, which is southwest of Chicago.)

Since I was not figuratively bleeding at this point Mr. O'Caine decided to plunge his verbal knife deeper into my psyche with the following question: 'How would you feel if a judge or another attorney called you a "Black Bitch?"' Since I did not gasp or blink following his crude remark he decided to make negative comments about my hair and dress.

(On the occasion of this writer's interview with Attorney Chatman, she was the epitome of a Vogue Magazine model with an ankle length black mink coat dramatically draped over her 5'10" frame.)

Mr. O'Caine never discussed any substantive issues about my qualifications for the job. I sat there in his office for minutes that seemed like hours in a state of disbelief. What was happening to me was incredulous. When his questioning appeared to be winding down I stood up and thanked him for his time and walked out.

I shared my Baker & McKenzie experience with several of my classmates. Their thoughts on how I should handle the matter varied. Some of them suggested that I should not do anything because it would ruin my whole career in that I would be labeled a troublemaker. Others told me if I went public with allegations on a firm as large as Baker and McKenzie I would be blackballed for life. On the other hand a number of people sincerely believed that I should lay down and play dead. However, an overwhelming majority thought that I should do something about the indignities that had been dumped on me.

My parents taught me early in life to always use my best judgement when confronted with a distasteful situation. Therefore, I felt obligated to write a letter detailing my experience to Dean Stone at the University of Chicago Law School and copying it to the managing partner at Baker and McKenzie.

I would have lost respect for myself if I had not taken a stand. As a result of my letter the Baker and McKenzie law firm was suspended from recruiting students at the University of Chicago Law School for one year. I have been told that the working environment at that firm for non-whites has improved dramatically. The reputation of the firm was tarnished when the contents of my letter was leaked to the Chicago Sun-Times by a person or persons unknown to me.

The legal profession did not have a monopoly on Jim Crow as seen through the eyes of Dr. Robert C. Stepto

Dr. Robert C. Stepto
Ph.D and M.D.

B.S., M.S., Ph.D and M.D. He shared the following views on segregation:

"The housing of Black patients in hospitals mirrored the Jim Crow patterns of our society at large. For example, at the Illinois Central Hospital, which is now Doctors Hospital of Hyde Park, Inc. at 5800 South Stony Island Avenue, historically Black patients were kept in the basement by agreement with the Illinois Central Railroad who owned the hospital. The Negro patients' beds were approximately four small rooms removed from where we performed autopsies on cadavers. This was a terrible situation.

There were segregated wards at the General Hospital in Washington, D.C. I recall when we made rounds at St. Elizabeth Hospital, a mental institution in the District of Columbia, they had floors for Blacks and floors for whites. Lying-In Hospital at the University of Chicago had the Max Epstein area, which housed Black patients on the south side of the building. The upper floor of the hospital was reserved for white patients.

Segregation was minimal at Cook County Hospital because of its heavy patient load. Lewis Memorial, like many other hospitals, dodged the segregation problem by placing Black patients in private rooms. At the South Chicago Hospital, the Black patients were an anomaly for

45

so long that they were simply accepted. Black and white wards existed for a long time. It was not until about 1969 or '70 that we began to see the open-bed policy practiced in Chicago hospitals.

Today you can walk through hospitals and find little discrimination in the assignment of beds. This is due to two pressures: Economic pressure from Blacks who can afford to pay for top medical service, and pressure from the courts and activists to end discrimination in health care. However, there are still some white doctors who refuse to permit their patients to share a room with a Black. Their motto is segregation yesterday, segregation today, segregation forever. I made some effort to alleviate segregation by appointing a white doctor from the Woodlawn Hospital to the Provident Hospital staff.

It's strange how I got on the staff at the Woodlawn Hospital by the back door. One of my patients was carried to the emergency room at the Woodlawn Hospital because she was bleeding profusely. The doctors there said that I was on staff, though I never had been. They called me and asked that I come over immediately to see this patient. While I was there they asked me whether I would join them. That is how I became the first Black doctor on the staff of Woodlawn Hospital.

A year later, John Harrod, who had been a resident in OB-GYN at the University of Chicago when I was studying pathology there, asked me to join the staff at South Chicago Hospital. The hospital was attempting to qualify for an accredited OB-GYN program. Since I had been board certified in OB-GYN since 1952 and John Harrod was also certified, we were directly responsible for South Chicago Hospital getting accreditation. I didn't have time to do a lot of work out there. I did some surgery and a few deliveries. At least some of my white peers had opportunities to see a Black physician perform under all kinds of circumstances. In 1968, I became chairman of the Department of Obstetrics and Gynecology at the Chicago Medical School. When the Chicago Medical School and Mt. Sinai merged, I was asked to become chairman at Mt. Sinai. The first day that I came on board, several white physicians decided they wanted to take their patients elsewhere. They moved their practices to Skokie, Highland Park and other North Shore locations. The majority of the staff supported me and I ran both programs.

Louis Armstrong, the father of the Jazz Trumpet.

Joe "Every Day I Get The Blues" Williams.

But, the meanest cut of them all was the intra racism game as practiced by Sammy Stewart in the spring of 1924. Stewart was the sophisticated quadroon society band leader at the mob-owned Sunset Café located at 35th and Calumet Avenue in Chicago, Illinois, he refused to give Louis Armstrong an audition because his skin was too dark. The prerequisite for an interview required that you meet the brown bag test. Roy Butler, a light skinned saxophone player in the orchestra, said Stewart dismissed Louis without ever making eye contact with him.

Joe Williams, the internationally famous singer with the Count Basie orchestra said the following about intra Black racism:

"In 1935 I formed The Jubilee Boys and we sang at local churches, weddings and funerals. Local bandleaders like Erskine Tate would encourage me to sing but they never paid me any money. My first professional break came from Johnny Long, a bandleader who called me one evening about 8:30 p.m. and said: "Man, I've got a gig at Bacon's Casino that starts at 10:00 p.m. and I will be by and pick you up within forty-five minutes." In the 1930s and early '40s, Johnny Long had one of the most popular club dance bands on the South Side of Chicago. I would sing beautiful ballads and waltzes with Johnny Long's orchestra but internally, I was in conflict with my role as a crooner. My image of ballad singers was "pretty boys" like Herb Jeffries, Billy Eckstine and other light-skinned fellows. I was reddish black and unattractive. I didn't fit the matinee idol mold of the 1930s. As a matter of fact, when I decided to give singing the old college try, I went to Charlie Glenn at the Rhumboogie, which was located at 343 East Garfield Boulevard. Charlie would not hire me because I was too dark. I also begged Joe Hughes, the owner of Joe's Deluxe at 6323 South Park

48

Avenue, for an opportunity to work. About two or three weeks before Christmas I would go to Joe Hughes and say: "Hey man, I need some money to get some presents for my mother and grandmother. Give me a job. I will work for twenty-five dollars a week."

Joe Hughes replied: "Aw, come on, man! I can't hire you for that little bit of money. You sing too good. You're just too good. You're overqualified."

"The truth is that my skin was too shady for both club owners. They were both light-skinned pretty boys. The darkest male singer ever to work for Charlie Glenn was "Gatemouth" Moore, and he was a teasing brown. My light-skinned Black brothers really whipped a racist color game on me. I was about twenty-five or twenty-six years old before I felt comfortable enough with my blackness to remove that cross of inferiority from my shoulders.

Nat "King" Cole, who was blacker than I, struck it big nationally through his recordings before most people outside the Black community knew he was Black. There was no television in those days, so you couldn't see him. As you remember, he had perfect diction, the kind my mother taught me to speak around the house. Since Nat Cole was darker than I was and making it big singing ballads, I felt that I should try my luck as a professional singer.
Nat Cole opened the doors for darker-hued male entertainers two decades before the "Black is beautiful" crusade of the 1960s."

Billy Eckstine, Vocalist and Bandleader

Charles Glenn and Dave "Bud Biliken" Kellum

Joe Hughes and Ken "Mr. Regal" Blewett

Nat "Wonder Boy" Cole

Langston Hughes, one of the great poets of the 20th Century.

The saddest reality of racism as seen through the eyes of a child is described poetically by Langston Hughes. To wit:

"Where is the Jim Crow section
On this merry-go-round
Mister, cause I want to ride?
Down South where I come from
White and colored
Can't sit side by side.
Down South on the train,
There's a Jim Crow car.
On the bus we're put in the back
But there ain't no back
To a merry-go-round!
Where's the horse
For a kid that's black?"

"Those German prisoners wouldn't eat
if I allowed you to sit near them."

Chapter VI

Go Back To Black
For The Facts Jack

The year 2000 marked the first time since the initial census was taken in 1790, that Americans were permitted to characterize themselves as a member of more than one race. In the 1990 census a citizen could only select from five racial options as opposed to one hundred and twenty-six possible ethnic combinations available leading into the final countdown for the year 2000. For example the Fred Hardwick family marked six boxes on their 2000 census form. He made a single check in the box for white Anglo-Saxon, and his wife marked the one for African American plus two checks each: white and African American for their teenage son and daughter. One's self-identity is blurred in that the individual will not be counted as Black or white. Blacks and other variations of minorities have been shamed into denying their own ethnicity and jump the broom to become a multiracial spook (slang for Negro) who sits behind the door.

Definitive racial figures are important because the census is used as a statistical yardstick for political redistricting wards and congressional districts, enforcing federal civil rights laws and voting rights, job discrimination, affirmative action and equal access to credit, mortgages and insurance. The negative side of the multiple choices made possible by the new census count will create a political loss of federal funds for African Americans, Asian Americans, and Native Americans. Those Blacks among us who have checked two boxes or more have lost these political, cultural and financial benefits.

If an African-American checks dual boxes for the 2000 census he or she is locked out of the census curve for ethnic empowerment until the 2010 census is taken. By 2010 hopefully the veil over their eyes will have been lifted and the brothers and sisters will begin to see the political light. Moreover, the new census method will dilute the community power base and there won't be any room at the ball for Cinderella and her fellow. The Blacks' struggle will have gone for naught despite the fact that thousands have died in the streets and on the battlefields of the world for over a period of two hundred years preceding the so called Emancipation Proclamation plus one hundred and thirty-five years thereafter. To prove this point, in 1990 African Americans represented 12 percent of the United States population, whereas it is projected that by the year 2020 if we continue to be the spooks who skip down Judy Garland's yellow brick road, the Black population count will have diminished to a ghostly 8 percent or less in the nation's census population.

In the year 2000, nearly 7 million Americans described themselves as multiracial. This figure reflects the increasing diversity of our nation where minority groups such as Blacks and Hispanics are growing significantly faster than the general white population.

One blocks out his culture by checking both the white and Black squares. The person does not achieve anything by such action other than a very personal ego trip. This can safely be said in the light of our nation's long history of viewing people as Black if they have even one drop of Black blood. The question to be answered is how does one measure type A and the various other combinations of blood types?

Thus checking two squares on the census questionnaire is an exercise in nonsense. Moreover, the tabulation by race in the year 2000 has added up to more than 100 percent because a large percentage of people are included in more than one category. A nation that is as obsessed with skin color and blood count as America is will never be genuinely "color blind". America's red, white and blue striped tent top will never be large enough to include Blacks and Native Americans as co-partners in the struggle for or realization of liberty, freedom and justice for "all" during the twenty-first century.

White Army doctors were serious about Black and white blood plasma during World War II. And for sometime thereafter white and Black blood banks were segregated like coach cars on a train south of the Mason-Dixon Line. Army doctors refused to give Black blood plasma to white wounded soldiers even when they were on the doorstep of death in a Jim Crow Army. They refused to give white blood plasma to Blacks under the same circumstance. The United States racist acts were paradoxical when one considers the fact that Dr. Charles Drew, a Black physician and chief of staff at Howard University Medical School in Washington, D.C. was one of the pioneers of the system for blood plasma preservation. The use of Jim Crow stored plasma saved several hundred thousand white soldiers' lives during World War II.

Dr. Charles Drew, M.D.
Pioneer in blood plasma preservation.
1904-1950

Only the Lord knows how many Black soldiers died because of such racist foolishness.

Blacks have lost lives, limbs and blood in every American battle including Bunker Hill in Boston, Mass. and when we were at war with Great Britain fighting to break the yoke that bound the American colonies to the king of England.

The United States Supreme Court overrode the civil rights laws in its separate but equal (which is a misnomer) ruling in the 1896 Plessey vs. Ferguson decision. It supported a racist premise. The court ruling was based solely on the color of one's skin and blood count. The separation of the two races while using public conveyances was not seen as unreasonable by the court. Even more obnoxious to the Fourteenth Amendment of the Constitution was the action of Congress when it passed a law in the first decade of the twentieth century, requiring separate schools for colored children in the nation's capitol. The congressional action paralleled the odiousness of the court's ruling.

Corporal Eddie Myles, a disabled World War II Veteran, observed when he returned to the United States in 1945 after fighting in the Pacific Theater of War, that sick and wounded colored war veterans were greeted with "for whites only" signs on all the toilet facilities above the basement level of the Walter Reed Veterans Hospital in Washington, D.C. Moreover, racism was so contagious in the District of Columbia that Blacks were practicing it among themselves. The writer saw evidence of it in 1943 on a circular being passed out on the Capitol Transit streetcar line that read: "rooms for rent to light-skin colored folks only."

During the era of "separate but equal" the problem of who was Black and who was white created serious difficulties for railroad carriers in that a considerable amount of litigation was initiated by whites who were mistaken for Blacks and forced to ride in the "for colored only" segregated cars. One of many cases, was the Chicago Rock Island and Pacific v. Allison, where a white woman was directed by a train conductor to ride in the "Colored" section of a railroad coach. The court decided that a jury in the process of estimating damage in such cases must consider the white woman's age, degree of refinement, and her mortification and humiliation if any, as well as her fear and nervous shock.

Utilizing the aforementioned standard, a Texas court reversed as excessive, a $1,000 judgement obtained by a white woman who was compelled to ride sixty miles in a Negro coach in the Missouri, K & T v. Ball case.

On the other hand, a Kentucky court approved an award of $3,750 in the Louisville and M.R.R. Co. v. Ritchell for a white woman required to ride in a Negro coach by a conductor who was insulting in his conduct and pushed her into the "Colored" car even after she declared she was white, thus causing her nervous shock and anguish. Confusion over who is a Negro will not be resolved under the 2000 census umbrella which permits one to pick all the colors in the rainbow to describe one's self.

In an America where race plays a central role on the political stage, the 2000 census will only broaden the debate. Many Hispanics include themselves in the "other race" category since many of them because of their dark skin and blood count cannot physically pass for white.

The Hispanic population is like a stew with everything in it. The Spanish speaking population in the United States is now 35.3 million and nearly equals the American Blacks, although dark skin people represent a healthy percentage among the Black Spanish-speaking folks from the Caribbean Islands and Latin American countries such as Cuba, Puerto Rico, Colombia, Panama, Costa Rica, Brazil and Nicaragua. Dark skin Republic Natives do not see themselves through a telescope as do white Cubans. Some Hispanics frequently say, "I am not Black but I am not white either." In the fifty states you were either Black or white. Anything else falls through the cracks of I don't know who I am except at election time.

Samuel Boute, a teacher in Chicago said census choice was less about politics and more about pride. He declared that he was an African American, and thus he checked one square because that was the way he was raised. His mother is a fair-skin Creole woman from New Orleans where his maternal grandfather rode on the back of the segregated *Streetcar Name Desire* even though he appeared to be a pure unadulterated white man. Because of the position that his foreparents took he exclaimed "I am proud to be an African American."

Many Creoles included themselves with those who checked several boxes because they did not see a clear category that included them. On the other hand Arab-

58

Americans have also argued unsuccessfully for their own race box on the census form. Arabs, like all dark skin people rode on the back of the bus and ate in segregated restaurants before 1956 unless they happened to wear a turban. In the 1930s the all time great heavyweight champion of the world, Joe Louis use to say during the 1930s to his opponents in the ring: "You can run but you can't hide." That adage is as applicable today as it was then.

The above photograph identifies four generations of Lloyd
Garrison Wheeler III's maternal family. Mr. Wheeler at this
writing in 2001 is age 94, he made the following observa-
tions about his family during a series of interviews with
this writer over a span of years. Wheeler said:

*"I knew and personally conversed with these family
members at various times. This photograph of them cov-
ers a period of 160 years from 1827 to 1987.*

*From left to right: Sarah Ann Wilhoite, my great-
grandmother, was born in slavery on the Wilhoite planta-
tion in Greene County, Tennessee. 1827-1920*
*Dora Henrietta Wilhoite, my grandmother, was also born in
slavery. 1858-1949*
Madge Ann Thomas, my mother. 1883-1980
Edwin Thomas Wheeler, my brother. 1917-1987
*(Edwin is the baby in the arms of my mother Madge
Thomas and he is also in the inset as a young man 25
years old.")*

Chapter VII

The Evolution of An African-American Family: 1800 to 2002

In the quiet of a hot summer afternoon on July 3rd, 1811 John Wheeler a tobacco plantation owner sat down with pen and paper at his roll-top desk. He held a pen made from the shaft of a red feather in his right hand and a cool mint julep heavily spiked with bourbon whiskey in his left hand as he wrote what he described as his last will and testament. Inasmuch as he declared the document to be his final will it automatically revoked all the other earlier codicils. The new will was signed in the presence of the following testators to wit: John C. Green, T. Wolfe, Joseph Nichtlin and George A. Thornton.

In the first paragraph of the bequeathal he said the following: *I, John Wheeler of the County of Culpeper in the state of Virginia, do make and constitute this document to be my last will and testament which is framed in the manner and form, prescribed by the Virginia state law. Hence, it is my will and desire that at my death all of my house Negroes be emancipated then and forever more. My executors shall remove or cause them to be removed to the state of Ohio within a space of twelve months or less after I have inhaled my final breath. I am sincerely hopeful that my Negroes will be able to enjoy their new state of liberty* unmolested.

President Thomas Jefferson

My house Negroes by name are: Polly, and her three children, Nancy, Abner, and Hiram ... I give and bequeath to my Negress Polly one brindle cow, one feather bed and furniture. I also bequeath to Polly sixty dollars, one male horse and twenty pounds of wool, together with all of their bedding and clothing, etc. (Master John Wheeler was the father of Polly's children.) Polly was a shapely teasing brown Negro beauty and unquestionably his concubine the same as Sally Hemings was President Thomas Jefferson's mistress and the mother of at least four of his children.

John Wheeler died in his sleep of natural causes in 1819 approximately eight years after the date of his final will, which had been signed on the day before the fourth of July, 1811. Polly Wheeler and her three children moved to Ohio pursuant to old man Wheeler's final directions however they made a slight detour enroute to Ohio by stopping briefly in Pennsylvania where her light and almost white, handsome son Hiram met and married a German girl named Juliet Ann Muller on April 17,1820, she was 21 and he was

A family in transition from Black to white. The photo was taken in 1902. These people were just two generations away from crossing the color lines.

26. Juliet's father was of Pennsylvania Dutch ancestry. The zebra couple had originally met at a Pennsylvania County Fair.

In Mansfield, Ohio where they settled, the Hiram Wheelers became active members of the State's Abolition Movement. They became conductors in the Underground Railroad. Sojourner Truth was a leader in the Underground movement. The railroad was actually a well-used beaten path to freedom for runaway slaves. Everything went well for the Wheelers in their abolition activities until December 1850 when the enactment of the Fugitive Slave Act became law with its accompanying kidnapping provision that enabled headhunters to reinslave free Negroes and take

63

**Sojourner Truth, an abolitionist.
"A Pilgrim for Freedom"**

them back to the bloodhound Negro hunting grounds in the states below the Mason-Dixon Line. Thus, to avoid the possibility of losing their own freedom which was a real possibility under the new law the Wheelers sold all the chattel they could not carry with them on the journey North to the terminal of the U n d e r g r o u n d Railroad which was located in Chatham, Canada. By 1850, the Wheelers had produced eight children including Lloyd Garrison Wheeler Sr. who was born May 29, 1848 and Robert Foster Wheeler whose natal day was on December 4, 1851.

Lloyd and Robert Wheeler received their primary and secondary education in both Chatham, Canada and Detroit, Michigan. Lloyd began reading the law in Detroit and formally enrolled in the Chicago College of Law on South Michigan Avenue shortly after migrating to Chicago with several of his siblings. On the other hand, Robert Foster Wheeler migrated back to the East Coast where he

64

Attorney Lloyd   **Rev. Robert Foster**
Garrison Wheeler   **Wheeler**
The Wheeler Brothers

enrolled at the Howard University Theological Seminary in

Washington, D.C. He had managed to pass the entrance examination to the university based on his proficiency in reading. Robert had not formally graduated from a secondary school, but when he graduated from the University June 22, 1877 at the top of his class and was immediately ordained at the First Congregational Church in Washington D.C.

In 1869 at the age of 21, Lloyd Garrison Wheeler became the first quasi-white Negro to pass the Illinois Bar. He accomplished this feat within six years after Abraham Lincoln signed the Emancipation Proclamation, freeing all slaves on January 1, 1863. A year before he became a lawyer he married (Sarah) Rayne Petit the niece of John

Jones, a very successful tailor and allegedly one of the wealthiest Black citizens in the state of Illinois.

John Jones was a native of Green County, North Carolina where he was a former slave and the love child of a German name Bromfield. His mother was a beautiful Black woman who answered to the surname of Jones. John purchased his own freedom and migrated to Illinois via Memphis, Tennessee. His accomplishments in Illinois were signaled by his appointment as a notary public by Governor Palmer of Illinois. He was also the first Negro to be elect-

John Jones, a leader in the fight against the Black code.   **Mary Jane Jones, the wife of John Jones.**

ed a member of the Board of Commissioners of Cook County as a member of the Fire Party in 1871. Mr. Jones died on April 22, 1879 at the age of 62. He was an abolitionist, a close friend of Frederick Douglass, John Brown, and Joseph Medill, who was a high profile Republican in addition to being the editor and business manager of the Chicago Tribune. Medill became the Mayor of Chicago following the 1871 Chicago Fire. Medill was also John

Joseph Medill, Editor of the Chicago Tribune and Mayor of Chicago in 1871.

Jones' political mentor. Chicago in the early 1870's did not offer any opportunities for a spanking brand new Negro lawyer. Therefore, Lloyd Garrison Wheeler, in 1870 at the age of 22 he went south to Arkansas and managed to get himself elected through his Republican political connection for a one year term as County Attorney of Pulaski County, and in 1871 he was appointed to serve as a Presidential Elector for the Union's Civil War hero General Ulysses S. Grant. Grant was elected President on the Republican ticket in 1872.

Lloyd Garrison Sr. and Rene Petil had seven children, their names and birth dates are as follows:

1872   John Jones "Pete " Wheeler
1877   Mabel Augusta Wheeler (Evans)
1878   Robert Foster Wheeler
1880   Lloyd Garrison Wheeler, Jr.
1881   Hiram Hannibal Wheeler

They also had 2 daughters who were stillborn.

Madge Anna Thomas who became Lloyd G. Wheeler Jr.'s mother, was born on a farm in Rockville, Indiana the day of our Lord December 3, 1883. Her father made his final transition in 1891 when she was only eight years old. Her mother remarried a Broadlands, Illinois

farmer named Gaines. This marriage changed her life forever in that she became an unwanted stepdaughter.

In December 1904 Wheeler's mother left her
Broadland, Illinois home in the company of her great-
grandmother Sarah Ann Wilhoite who was born in slavery
on the Wilhrite plantation in Green County, Tennessee on
June 19, 1827. Shortly after the turn of the last century,
Sarah Ann and her husband Ernest made a trek west hoping
to stake out a land claim in the Oklahoma Territory.

On June 9, 1905 while in Oklahoma Madge Anna
Thomas met and married Hiram Hannibal Wheeler Sr. he
had been a student and a member of the University of
Illinois football team in
Champaign, Urbana.

On August 26, 1907,
in St. Joseph, Missouri,
Lloyd Garrison Wheeler
III became the first child
of Madge Anna and Hiram
Wheeler.   Hiram   was
employed as a teacher at
Lincoln University in St.
Joseph, Missouri. It was a
low paying job that did not
appear to have a bright
future for a man with a
wife and son plus twin
daughters in the basket.
Opportunity   knocked

**Booker T. Washington,
founder of Tuskegee
Institute.**

when he got an offer
through his grandfather
Attorney Lloyd Garrison
Wheeler to join the teach-
ing staff at Booker T. Washington's Institute in Tuskegee,
Alabama. At Tuskgee he found the social life richer in that
he met most of the movers and shakers of that period how-

ever, his salary was thinner than a fried slice of bacon.

In 1909 despite the social attractions at Tuskegee Hiram gave up teaching and bought a small farm in Southern Wisconsin. He made this judgement call based on his wife's background and knowledge of farming. A disastrous forest fire cut that dream short. The road he took out of the dilemma was to go south back to the University of Illinois where he was well known and admired as a football hero. He was offered and accepted a job as a recreation director for the YMCA. The program was geared toward World War I recruits and returning war veterans. Shortly before the war ended on November 11, 1918, Hiram Wheeler was hit by a nationwide plague of influenza and double pneumonia. Hiram Wheeler died on October 16, 1918, which was less than a month before World War I ended. His eldest child Lloyd G. Wheeler was only eleven years old. The future for widow Madge Ann and her five young ones was two steps west of hell.

In 1923, Madge Anna and her basketball team of five moved to Chicago where they found other members of his late father's family who willingly offered aid and assisted the widow woman and her five children. Some years later the widow met and married Paul Scott a widowed neighbor. That marriage lasted until Scott made his transition some years later. Madge Anna died in 1980 just before her 97th birthday. She kept her promise in that she devoted her entire life to her children.

Lloyd G. Wheeler her eldest son followed in his father's footsteps by enrolling in and graduating from the University of Illinois in 1932. It took him seven years to get his sheepskin because he worked part time washing dishes and sweeping floors in order to pay his tuition. His primary part time job was at the Liberty Life Insurance where he started working as an office boy in 1923 two years before graduating from Hyde Park High School. In 1991, he retired as the President of the Company where he started

**Lloyd G. Wheeler, civic leader and the President of Supreme Life Insurance .
Mr. Wheeler's grandfather married John Jones' adopted daughter and they inherited his property at 119 North Dearborn Street, fifty feet north of Madison Street after the old man died in 1879.**

working as a boy of sixteen.

In 2001 Lloyd Garrison Wheeler, Jr. is the oldest surviving child of Hiram Hannibal Wheeler and Madge Anna Thomas. At age 94 Mr. Lloyd G. Wheeler is still in good health and resides in the expanded Bronzville in the Chatham area on the south east side of Chicago.

Ebony publisher John H. Johnson and former chairman of Supreme Life Insurance Company was a high school mate of this writer and he has consistently given Lloyd G. Wheeler high marks for dedication and performance as an officer of their company.

Left to right: Judge Sidney Jones, John H. Johnson, chairman of Johnson Publishing Company, Truman Gibson, Sr., former chairman of Supreme Life and Congressman Ralph Metcalfe.

71

**A Native American
Sioux Nation**

Chapter VIII

Have The Red Man's Casinos Magnetized the White Boys?

Green American dollar bills are the world's greatest attraction. New financial opportunities for Native Americans in the gambling business have prompted some white boys to want to become red men. There are white folks in the state of Connecticut who are working overtime to prove that they have Indian ancestors. As a matter of fact there is a 50% increase in "pretenders" and "wannabe" Indians. Many paleface brothers are attempting to high jump over the reservation fence and slip into the Red Men's moccasins.

The Indian population in the New England states has increased from 6,700 in 1990 to more than 9,600 in the year 2000 according to the latest census count. On the other hand, nationally there are 4.1 million white and Black

73

Americans who have marked the census questionnaire as part Native American, thus doubling the 1990 figure. The American Indian population numbers have soared far beyond anything that can be explained by birthrate. Experts and tribal officials believe that the new millennium gold rush to become a tribal member of an Indian nation is the result of a new found Buffalo which today is gambling casino revenue.

In the year 2001 the Mashantucket Pequot Indians are the wealthiest tribe in the United States, their Foxwoods casino is reputed to be the largest in the world. This achievement did not come to them without extended legal expense and many brutal court battles with their white neighbors who still feel that the Indians have extended their boundaries beyond what was originally staked out in the 1880s as their reservation.

Christopher Columbus

The monies that made Foxwoods Casino possible came from some Malaysian gambling investors who provided them with several hundred million dollars for a piece of the casino action. Foxwoods is truly a modern Cinderella story in that the cash cows that made their growth possible actually came via a vehicle that was a world away from Connecticut. In the writer's opinion there is more than a kindred spirit between the Indians of the Pacific and those who met Christopher Columbus and his crew when they landed in the New World on the Pinta, the Nina and the Santa Maria.

Under our Federal Law, the nation's Indian tribes

are permitted to make their own rules about those who may be considered wigwam worthy. Some Indian nations require a certain blood quantum the same as American whites have used historically in determining whether an individual is Black or white and then there are those who use old census reports and still others rely on historical documents to determine Indian lineage.

According to studies in 1896 by the John Hopkins University in Baltimore, Maryland entitled *Slavery and Servitude in the Colony of North Carolina*, the theme of the study dealt with the commonality of intermarriage between Indians and Negroes. In fact, bonafide claims for freedom were made by many Negro slaves who could prove Indianhood on the maternal side of their forbearers. Positive proof of one having Indian maternal genes was considered prima facie evidence that such a Negro was entitled to freedom. Claims of Indianhood by Negroes was further supported by various gubernatorial proclamations and acts of assembly which decreed that Indians were not to be subjected to perpetual and hereditary servitude. Undoubtedly the majority of slaves with Negro-Indian blood never attempted to obtain their freedom via their Indian ancestry.

A young Native American.

In Tahlequan, Oklahoma on a daily basis, some hopeful persons with pale white skin and sky blue eyes would present themselves along with some convoluted evidence to Lela Ummertekee, the tribal registrar in an attempt to fulfill an inspired dream of becoming rich by claiming their American Indian ancestry. Most of them like this writer could not prove anything more substantial than what my maternal grandmother told me many moons ago. She declared until breath left her body that my great-grandfather was a Cherokee Indian. Unlike some of those white dreamers I just never had the nerve to try and sell her truth to anybody outside of my immediate family.

There are individuals who in their effort to enroll in the Cherokee nation have presented such things as X-ray film of their heads purporting to show Indian cheekbones. Other "wannabees" have literally scraped patches of white skin from their arms in the presence of the Indian registrar as evidence that a distant ancestor was a Native American.

The gold stampede that is presently taking place on the Indian Reservation with the aid of federal courts and the United States Congress is raising more questions than answers. Historically, Indians have had a deep mistrust of Federal officials in that they were the ones who expropriated their land and bunched them as a class into small land pockets that became known as reservations following the Civil War.

Looking backward in history at the Delaware tribe of Indians who were the first in the nation to be federally recognized for treaty rights that turned out to be counterfeit in that they vanished during the 19th and 20th century like smoke rings in the night. The treaties among other things are the reason that many Native Americans still say: "The white man speaks with a fork tongue."

The Lumbees, a tribe of 40,000 in North Carolina open their enrollment for only a few months every three or four years because they are swamped with thousands of requests from those who want to prove their Native American heritage. Many of the applicants are descendants of the Lumbees. Their families moved away from the reservation five or six decades ago and now their second generation offsprings are returning to seek jobs and opportunities which were not available before the last decade of the twentieth century.

Are the 21st Century paleface invaders coming to deliver gifts of respect or diseased treated blankets that literally almost wiped out a whole generation of Native Americans? If the latter is found to be true, the present movement would go down in history as the second round of biological warfare on this continent.

Elouise Cobell, seen here in front of an oil well on the Blackfeet Indian Reservation near Browning, Mt., Wednesday Sept. 8,1999, says she remembers her parents wondering why they weren't getting paid regularly for letting others use their land to farm and drill for oil. Now as the lead plaintiff in a class-action lawsuit over mismanagement of Indian trust accounts, Cobell is taking on the federal government in an effort to reform the system responsible for distributing royalties and lease money to Indians for the use of their land.

Chapter IX

Cobell's Bow and Arrow vs. The USA'S Automatic Rifles

Mrs. Elouise Cobell is a 55 year old 5 feet 4 inch Blackfeet Indian woman who set out at the age of 25 to correct a one hundred and fourteen year old financial betrayal that is evident by the misuse of billions of dollars that are long overdue to Native Americans from the coffers of the United States Treasury Department.

The subterfuge for the massive Indian betrayal began in 1887, when the U.S. government decided to breakup the tribal reservations for land hungry white frontiersmen and their families. The quid pro quo for the transaction according to The Bureau of Indian Affairs was based on the fact that individual Indians were to be conveyed 11 million acres of land divided into 80 to 160 acres. As trustee, the United States Treasury took legal title, to all the acreage that rightfully belonged to 300,000 Indians who became beneficiaries of the trust. Thus, until the present day the money and the land are still controlled by the Interior Department's Bureau of Indian Affairs and the United States Treasury Department.

To make bad matters worse, Indians were not permitted to lease or sell their own property without the approval stamp of the United States government. Thus, with one swoop of a pen federal officials negated all of the red man's fee simple property rights. The fraudulent agreement also prohibited the Indians from making deals with corporate companies for logging, grazing, quarrying rights or negotiating leases with timber, agriculture, oil, natural gas and mineral speculators.

The Department of the Interior politicians anointed themselves with the sole power to make lead cinched deals with their political contributors. The United States Treasury also became trustee of the money that was collected in each transaction. The Indians' individual compensation was to be based on the acres of land that had been conveyed by each individual family to the trust.

The Bureau of Indian Affairs (BIA) which is a subsidiary of the Department of Interior was in charge of channeling the money through the United States Treasury Department, and the Treasury in turn was suppose to process the checks and mail out the individual checks to the beneficiaries of the trust. This latter act is where the scheme purposely fell through the cracks of the bureaucratic floor in that the Blackfeet Indians never received more than a teardrop of any portion of the billions of dollars that had been long overdue. The Native Americans were further blindsided in that they were not privileged with any knowledge of how much money had been collected in each lease deal or the names of the vendees.

Cobell, the solver of the Native American Indians' financial puzzle was born in a lean-to hut in 1945 on a

Blackfeet Indian reservation in the state of Montana. Little Miss Cobell enrolled in a one-room country elementary school on the Blackfeet Indian reservation in 1950. Her family lived in a shanty that was phoneless, wireless and without running water. The only toilet facilities in their very humble abode were bedpans, slop jars and an outdoor privy in the backyard. They took turns in the use of a Sears, Roebuck and Co., 1920 portable copper lined bathtub for their daily sponges and baths.

After Elouise Cobell finished elementary school, she went to a high school that was located some 50 miles round trip by bus from the Indian reservation. After graduating from high school where she was an excellent student she enrolled in a two-year business college in Great Falls, Montana where she majored in accounting. She chose the accounting field as a profession because she felt that it would be helpful to her in untangling her people's financial affairs with the United States Treasury Department and the Bureau of Indian Affairs.

She recalls when she was a little girl the elders of the tribe would come to her house and meet with her father. She frequently overheard heated conversations about what the government was doing with their money. The shame of her people's financial betrayal was implanted in her brain as a child and hovered over her head like a dark cloud into early adulthood and beyond.

In 1976, the Black Feet Tribal Council appointed her to the position of tribe treasurer because of her accounting background and the general interest she displayed in Indian affairs. She had had some work experience earlier in the local BIA office in a student workstudy program. The young lady saw firsthand how the Bureau of Indian Affairs' white officials treated her people like sticky red clay under the soles of their shoes. She vividly remembers seeing her people sitting in the BIA office all day long on uncomfortable hardwood benches waiting to be served. There were no inside restroom facilities for the Blackfeet Indians because there was an unwritten gentleman's agreement that the indoor plumbing was to be used by white folks only. Cobell recalls witnessing the sad sight of the most down-trodden of her people begging with maplike lines across their foreheads and frowns of sadness on their faces and tears in their eyes as they pleaded for money, food, and clothing for their children.

As the tribe treasurer, Cobell tried to get a handle on everything. Initially she tried to work with the local and regional Bureau of Indian Affairs (BIA) offices where she was repeatedly stonewalled. Her next move was to turn her attention to the Department of Interior in Washington, D.C. Her batting average in the District of Columbia did not improve.

In 1989, she arranged to meet with Representative Mike Synar, an Oklahoma Democrat with a large Native American constituency. He gave her an audience and in turn arranged a meeting for her with officials of the Office of Management and Budget during the first Bush Administration. In addition to Cobell, a prominent banking attorney named Dennis Gingold was also invited to Washington, D.C. to attend the meeting. At that meeting a lot of heat was generated but very little of substance was accomplished except Cobell remembered Gingold saying at one point during a lively discussion between him and a pla-toon of government lawyers, "I am amazed you guys haven't been sued."

In 1994, five years after Cobell's initial meeting with Congressman Synar, he was able to persuade a Congressional Committee during the Clinton Administration to authorize a presidential appointment of a special trustee to provide a full accounting of the monies owed the Blackfeet, Cherokees, Apaches, Winnebagos and other Indian tribes located west of the Mississippi River.

Sharp Nose, Arapho

Satanta, Kiowa warrior

Artistic conception of "Custer's Last Stand" in the Dakotas, June 25,1876.

The Trail Of Tears as depicted by the artistic rendering above was a forced exodus from North Carolina to Oklahoma. The displacement of the Southeastern Indians took place between 1820 and 1840. The great, great, great, great, grandmother of Carol J. Gallagher the 45 year old Cherokee Indian elected Suffragan Episcopal Bishop in the Diocese of Southern Virginia in 2001, was one of the displacees who walked The Trail of Tears in that shameful time. The Bishop's mother is Elizabeth Walking Stick a member of the Cherokee Nation.

Stu-Mick-O-Sucks,
The Buffalo's Back Fat,
Head Chief of the Blackfeet

Crow King, Sioux

Short Bull, Sioux

Long Dog, Sioux

Geronimo, the most feared Indian.

General Crook's famous scouts fought Apache
bands that remained hostile and helped track
down Geronimo. Their reward was to be sent off
to prison in Florida.

Dr. Martin Luther King
Nobel Prize Recipient

A banking executive by the name of Paul Homan was appointed to straighten out the Indians' financial mess. Bruce Babbitt, President Clinton's newly appointed Secretary of the Interior appeared to go out of his way to throw roadblocks in Homan's way. In disgust Homan quit the job and accused Babbitt of stripping him of the authority to give creditable performance. Both Secretary Babbitt and Attorney General Janet Reno treated Cabell like a pariah. Hence, she came to the conclusion that a lawsuit against the Washington establishment was her only recourse. Recalling what Attorney Dennis Gingold had said in the 1989 meeting with the OMB people about a lawsuit, she decided to hire him to represent the Indians. Gingold told her he was not a rainmaker and that such a suit would be extremely expensive. Cabell told Dennis that she would get the money somehow and advised him to get the show on the road. She then began her fundraising efforts by soliciting monies from a number of foundations and she thereby successfully managed to raise almost eight million dollars. Elouise Cobell also received the John D. MacArthur Foundation "genius award" which was a personal grant for 300,000 dollars. She promptly deposited all of her grant money in the pot for the benefit of the Native Americans' struggle in the same fashion that Dr. Martin Luther King did with his Nobel Prize award money.

President Warren G. Harding
1920-1924

Chapter X

A Blood Red Sky Was Over The Potomac In 2002

The mismanagement of the Indians' trust funds by the United States government officials parallels the scandals of the Teapot Dome (1923) rip-off, which brewed to a boiling point during President Warren G. Harding's Administration. The golf playing president had more than his share of parasite clubhouse friends. It is unfortunate that this president's appointed lovers of the green thought that holding public office was a license to steal. Charles Forbes of the Veterans Administration served hard time in federal prison after being convicted of fraud and bribery in connection with government contracts. Another partner in crime was Thomas W. White, the custodian of alien property, he was jailed for accepting bribes. Attorney General Harry Daugherty was deeply implicated in bribery schemes

95

Harding politicking with a baby in arms on the golf course.

and other fraudulent acts; he escaped going to prison by pleading the fifth amendment of the constitution and thus exercising his right to refuse to testify against himself. The most infamous case among the many during the Harding Administration was the one that followed a congressional inquiry in 1923 and 1924. The hearing uncovered the fact that Secretary of Interior Albert Fall had accepted bribes to lease government controlled Indian owned properties to private oil companies. For his role in the Teapot Dome Scandal - a name derived from a Wyoming oil well reserve that had been leased to the Mammouth Oil Company. Fall was fined $100,000 (which was comparable to a million dollars in today's currency) he also spent a year serving hard time in jail, the man was the first cabinet officer ever caught with both of his hands in a bucket of red paint, but he was not the last.

Another name that comes to mind for being inducted into the hall of ill fame is Spiro Agnew, the former tough talking governor of Maryland and subsequently vice president in the Richard M. "I ain't no crook" Nixon Administration. Agnew resigned from the office of vice president after pleading no contest to charges of income tax evasion and the acceptance of bribes.

Vice President   **President Richard**
Spiro Agnew   **Milhouse Nixon**

By fast forwarding to August 2001 and high jump-
ing over a number of lesser scandals the writer discovered
that the Department of Treasury, under the second Bush
Administration meted out some feather pillow whacks on
the hands of a group of government attorneys appointed
during the President William Clinton era and subsequently
found guilty of wrongdoing for attempting to cover up
information about the shredding of 162 large cardboard
boxes containing historical financial records related to the
trust accounts of American Indians.

The Department of Treasury tried to keep the details
of the scandal away from the eyes and ears of the taxpaying
public and the Congress moreover they refused to dole out
punishment commensurate with the seriousness of the white
collar crime. Two of the lawyers did not receive any discipline because they left the department and went into private
practice in October 2000 whereas, the other four attorneys
were given a slap on the wrist and ordered to take private
counseling and attend some management training sessions.

According to court documents and some internal

reports, the attorneys were actually aware of the record shredding that took place at a Department of Treasury warehouse facility in January 1999 at Hyattsville, Maryland. The lawyers set on their hands until May 1999 when they finally informed the court of the destroyed records. The episode of concealment took place in spite of the fact that they were under court orders to produce the material. Treasury Secretary Robert Rubin and other top Clinton officials were slapped with contempt fines by U.S. District Judge Royce Lamberth for failing to comply with his orders.

Judge Lamberth appointed Federal monitor Joseph S. Kieffer III who later documented the shocking pattern of noncompliance and deception by both the Interior and Justice Departments.

The Kieffer report laid bare before the eyes of the court the fact that the Interior Department had been telling the court and congress a big bunch of white lies for eighteen consecutive months about the progress that was not being made in accounting for all the money that had passed in and out of the individual Indian trust accounts.

Elouise Cobell said: *After more than five years of litigation, many of us are shocked at the government's shameful behavior in this case. This is our government, that is routinely stonewalling and lying to the court, Congress and us about our money, which the government has been stealing from my people for more than 100 years.*

On December 21, 1999 Judge Lamberth issued his Trial One opinion: He found that the government had breached its trust responsibilities to the Indians, thus he ordered the government to file quarterly reports detailing its efforts to reform the system, he further ruled that the court would retain jurisdiction over the system for at least five years. This latter order solicited muffled screams.

On August 16, 2000 the plaintiffs' lawyers asked the judge to hold Interior Secretary Babbitt in contempt for retaliating against a Bureau of Indian Affair's employee by the name of Mona Infield, because she had crossed the line and provided evidence damaging to the government's case. Special master Alan Balarian on February 21, 2001 recommended new contempt proceedings against Bruce Babbitt, Kevin Gover and eight other Interior officials, concluding that there was sufficient evidence to show that the Department of Interior officials had indeed retaliated against the BIA whistle-blower, Mona Infield, a Native American.

In April, Special Master Balarian issued an opinion finding the Federal Reserve track record on trust document preservation "abysmal" and "profoundly troubling." Balarian's report was comprised of incriminating documents in at least 29 of the 37 Federal branches.

On August 16, 2001 - the Justice Department's Office of Professional Responsibility informed Judge Lamberth that it had investigated the Judge's findings of "lack of good faith, cover-up and misconduct" by government attorneys and would submit its report to the court soon.

The plaintiffs' lawyers filed a motion in August 2001 asking Judge Lamberth to set January 8, 2002 as the date for trial on Phase II - and give an accounting to determine how much is owed by the government to the individual trust beneficiaries.

Joseph S. Kieffer III, the monitor said that a new court date was not enough, inasmuch as the Indian Trust Fund was still mired. "The usual cry that it did not happen on our watch is no longer a defense." As a matter of fact that story does not hold water and was clearly demonstrated in the 41 page report submitted to U.S. District Judge Royce C. Lamberth by the monitor.

The monitor Kieffer said: Interior managers, in a series of quarterly reports to a federal judge maintained that progress was being made, failed to provide a truthful, accu-

99

rate, and complete picture of the status of the reforms. Joseph S. Keiffer III, the monitor further said that Interior Secretary Gale A. Norton must share responsibility for the trust problem - even though they were decades in the making and that Norton had assumed office in January 2001 when she was appointed by the newly elected President George W. Bush. The reasoning for not letting Norton off the hook was justified because she had continued to rely upon the guidance of the same longtime managers who had had years to fix the system.

The 43 page report to Judge Lamberth should be the centerpiece for putting an outside receiver in charge to clean up the mess. The royalties from the Indian owned land generates monies that are approximately 500 million dollars a year, and more than 70 billion during the life of the trust.

A summary of the report issued during the week of October 15, 2001 reads as follows:

The government's three-year-old plan to fix the broken trust fund "may not be capable of repair" because Secretary of Interior Gale Norton has failed to take responsibility, a court monitor charged in a report highly critical of the Bush administration on Tuesday October 17, 2001.

Although numerous management problems existed before Norton took office nine months ago, they have "increased in severity" under her watch, said Joseph S. Kieffer III. Instead of supporting her top trust fund official Tom Slonaker, she and senior aides have rejected his advice and subjected him to "questioning," thereby undermining his authority throughout the department, he added.

And even though Norton has taken credit for taking steps to "streamline" trust reform, these efforts are inadequate, continued Kieffer. A new trust fund office, a special secretarial order and a $1 million effort to have an outside management consulting firm assess the government's capabilities are destined to fail because she has not addressed key reform issues that have been made evident to her in recent months, he has concluded. "There is no one in charge of trust reform operations," wrote Kieffer in the 30-page report. "There is no one who knows what is necessary or how to correct trust reform management, communications, and systems problems to bring about successful trust reform."

Kieffer's caustic criticism comes after the Interior turned in its latest trust fund status report. Without approval from a federal judge, the government submitted it a month late, citing a need to clear up concerns raised by Slonaker, a Clinton appointee retained by the Bush administration to oversee the trust accounts of an estimated 300,000 American Indians throughout the country.

But according to Kieffer and other court documents, Norton did little -- if anything at all -- to respond to Slonaker's reservations. Instead, her lawyers, Solicitor Bill Myers and senior management did all they could to avoid taking responsibility, said Kieffer. The result, wrote Kieffer, was that Norton "verified an untruthful, inaccurate, and incomplete" status report covering the months of May, June and July 2001. "No senior DOI official would touch that report with a ten-foot pole," he added.

Already having cited Norton and a number of other officials in their court filings, a lawyer for the plaintiffs in the Cobell v. Norton lawsuit said they would seek sanctions against government attorneys and senior management for "aiding and perpetrating a fraud on the court."

In particular, said Dennis Gingold, government attorneys have engaged in "unethical" conduct worthy of fines and potential disbarment.

Part Two: A Gallery of Portraits In Various Shades of Black

Sunday Sharp

The Gingham Girl

A Young Child of Negro and
Indian Heritage.

The Cute One

Mama's Little Man

The Lady Is Dressed to Kill in Her Holiday Outfit

The Violin Teacher

A Lady in Waiting

Three Generations

The Latest Style of the Period Was Baggy Knee-Breeches and a Frock Coat in 1888

An Ex-Union Soldier

The Soapbox Orator

**America's Original Harvard
Black Scholar**

113

Believe Me When I Say That I Know I Know

I Know I Am Cute

In A Blue Mood

A Full Bodied Lady Accentuating a Polka Dot Dress

The Young Professional

The Hat

The Profile

The Political Conqueror

The Guest Of Honor

Quiet Please

He Failed Being White By Two Ounces

The Preacher Man

She Had Sky Blue Eyes

A Dog Is a Man's Best Friend

A Graduate in the 1890 Class

**She Passed For White As a Salesgirl In a Major
Downtown Department Store.**

The Sophisticated Lady Of The Gay Nineties

The Greatest Contralto of the 20th Century

The Musician

She Passed For White By Day

A Bustle Dress On A Full Figured Woman

An Evening Gown Without The Bustle

The Widower

The Widow Woman

The Ivy Leaguer

A Man of Few Words

The High School Teacher

The Mathematics Instructor

The Reverend

The Preacher's Wife

The Sport

The Vision Of Glamour

A Classy Lady

A Gentleman of Means

A Fashionably Dressed Homemaker

The Haberdasher

The Boarding School Matron

First Cousins

Friends Forever

Four Generations of a Proud Family

**A Bike Ride on a Pleasant Sunday Afternoon In
1890**

Lean On Me

A Woman of Distinction

The Banker

The Socialite

Miss Sassy

The Beautiful Bride

The Landlady

A Lady of Substance

On His Best Behavior

Daddy's Little Girl

The Masonic Brother

The College Freshman

A Woman In Black

A Darling of The Twenties

Simply Irresistible

Harlem Flappers

A 1910 Fireman and His Young Daughter

The Aspiring Young Businessman

The Politician

The Surgeon

The Educator

An Itinerant Preacher

A Great Tenor

The Entrepreneur

The Harvard Man

The Political Iron Man

The Trailblazer

A Sunday Afternoon at The Sunset Hill Country Club

The Protester

A Union Soldier

The Colonel who Graduated from West Point in 1889

A Captain in WWI

A WWI Colonel Who Was the Soldiers' Soldier

The Buck Private

A Captain in the 332nd Flight Group

A WWII Army Medical Officer

They Never Clipped His Wings

A WWII Coast Guard Captain

The First Black General in the United States Army

A WWII Army Wac

An Officer in the 705th Tank Destroyers Battalion

Commander of the Eighth Infantry of Illinois

One of the Angels at Fort Huachuca, Arizona

The First Black Brigadier General in The United States Air Force

A Flight Leader in the 999th Fighter Squadron

**The Commanding Officer of the 184th Field
Artillery**

**He Did It By the Numbers From the ROTC to Four
Star General**

Bibliography

Interviews:

*Baker, Elmore, age 92, June 12, 1977

*Dickerson, Earl B., age 95, August 21, 1977 and various dates in 1978, '79, '80, and '81

+Duster, Alfreda M. Barnett, age 73, July 10, 1977

+Evans, Lovelyn J., age 82, August 4, 1977

*Ginnell, Anna Mary, age 94, July 29, 1977 and August 21, 1977.

+Lafontant, Jewel, age 58, July 23, 1981

+Mead, B. Ripley, Jr., age 56, June 10, 1969

+Mead, B. Ripley, Sr., age 79, June 10, 1969

*Ragland, John, age 96, April 13, 1980

*Travis, Mittie, age 93, June 12, 1977 and various other dates through 1989

+Wheeler, Lloyd, III, age 94, August 14, 1977 and various dates through 2001

*1or both parents were born in slavery
+grandparents were slaves

Books:

Adams, Russell L. Great Negroes Past and Present. Afro-American Publishing Company, Chicago, 1913.

Ball, Edward. Slaves In The Family . Ballentine Books, New York, 1998.

Bell, Derrick. Racism and American Law. Little Brown and Company, Boston, 1980.

Cates, Gwendolen. Indian Country Grove Press, New York, 2001.

Chase - Riboud, Barbara. Sally Hemings. Ballentine Books, New York, 1994.

Debo, Angie. The History of the Indian in the United States. United of Oklahoma Freed Press, Norman, 1970.

De Brown. Bury My Heart At Wounded Knee: An Indian History of the American West. Henry Holt and Company, New York, 1970.

Dumond, Dwight Lowell. Anti-Slavery: The Crusade For Freedom In America. University of Michigan Press, Ann Arbor, 1961.

Franklin, John Hope. From Slavery to Freedom. Alfred A. Knopf, New York: 1947.

Frazier, E. Franklin. Black Bougeoisie. The Free Press, Glencoe, 1957.

Graham, Lawrence Otis. Our Kind of People. Harper-Collins Publishers, New York, 1999.

Hamilton, Charles V. Adam Clayton Powell Jr. Athenum, New York, 1991.

Hansen, Henry Harold. Costume Calvacade. Methuen and Co. LTD., London, 1961.

Major, Gerri and Doris E. Saunders. Black Society. Johnson Publishing Co. Inc., Chicago, 1976.

McKissick, Floyd. 3/5 Of A Man. The MacMillan Company, New York, 1969.

Perry, Mark. Lift Up Thy Voice From Slaveholders to Civil Rights Leader. Viking Press, New York City, 2001.

Travis, Dempsey J. Autobiography of Black Jazz. Urban Research Press, Chicago, 1983.

Travis, Dempsey J. Racism American Style. Urban Research Press, Chicago, 1991.

Travis, Dempsey J. Racism, Round 'n' Round It Goes. Urban Research Press, Chicago, 1998.

Travis, Dempsey J. Views From The Back Of The Bus During WWII and Beyond. Urban Research Press, Chicago, 1995.

Travis, Dempsey J. The Duke Ellington Primer. Urban Research Press, Chicago, 1996.

Travis, Dempsey J. The Louis Armstrong Odyssey. Urban Research Press, Chicago, 1997.

Turner, Glennette Tilley. The Underground Railroad in Illinois. : Newman Educational Publishing, Glen Ellyn, 2001.

Tuttle, William M., Jr., Mary Beth Norton, Howard P. Chudacoff, et al. A People And A Nation. Houghton Mifflin Company, Boston, 1994.

Winfield, Erma. Savannah Brown. Publishers Group, Toluca Lake, California, 1994.

Wieneck, Henry. The Hairstons: An American Family in Black & White. St. Martins, New York:, 1998.

Newspapers:

Not the Last of This Tribe: Mohegans, Granted U.S. Recognition, Want a Casino. New York Times, March 24, 1924.

University Observes Its One Hundred and Fifth Commencement. Howard University School of Religion The News, June-July, 1973. Vol. 33, No. 3.

Mohawks Ask Cuomo to Join Peace Effort: Rival Factions Battle Over Issue of Casinos. New York Times, April 28, 1990.

2 Mohawks Killed in Feud Over Reservation Gambling. New York Times, May 2, 1990.

Indian Reservation Sealed Off After 2 Killings. New York Times, May 3, 1990.

Bibliography

Mohawk Reserve Quiet as Officials Meet. New York Times, May 4, 1990.

Mohawks' Border World Of Violence and Tradition. New York Times, May 5, 1990.

Whose Law Applies When Lawlessness Rules on Indian Land? New York Times, May 6, 1990.

Mohawks Mourn Victim Of Reservation Violence. New York Times, May 7, 1990.

Uncle Tom Lives; Mostly In Those Old Movies Shown on Cable Channels. Chicago Tribune, June 21, 1992.

Casinos Putting Tribes at Odds. New York Times, January 13, 1994.

Legalizing of Casinos Gains in Albany: Opposition Weakens as Gambling Spreads Throughout the Nation. New York Times, February 7, 1994.

Indian Chief and Waterbury's Mayor Announce Plan for a Casino. New York Times, March 4, 1994.

A James Bond With $100 Tries Out a Tribal Casino. New York Times, March 8, 1994.

Recognized As a Nation: Mohegans May Build State's 2d Casino. New York Times, March 8, 1994.

Casino Dreams After a Federal Nod To the Mohegans. New York Times, March 20, 1994.

Defenders of Jefferson Renew Criticism of DNA Analysis Linking Him to Slaves Child. January 7, 1999.

Fighting For Space At The Jefferson Family Table, New York Times, September 2, 1999.

A Black Child Under Hitler Recalls An Amazing Life. Chicago Sun Times, December 5, 1999.

A More Colorful Country. Chicago Sun-Times, March 12, 2001.

Media Release: Multiple Race Identities Most Common Among Children, Nonwhite Populations. Minnesota Planning, May 29, 2001.

Color and Culture Clash in Jazz Age. Chicago Tribune, June 10, 2001.

Historians Preserve Stops on a Track to Freedom. New York Times, July 10, 2001.

Interior Department Misled Court On Reforms, Report Says. The Washington Post, August 10, 2001.

Report Rips Interior Department. Chicago Sun-Times, October 10, 2001.

Report Rips Interior Department. Chicago Sun-Times, October 17, 2001.

With Growth In Gambling; Casinos Create Bitter Divisions Among Indians. New York Times, October 28, 2001.

Indian Woman Is Episcopal Bishop. New York Times, November 11, 2001.

Magazines:

Between Two Races. Negro Digest, February 1962.

U.S. President Thomas Jefferson Fathered Child With Slave, DNA Study Shows. Jet Magazine, November 16, 1998.

Total Lack of Trust. Insight, August 25, 2001.

The Broken Promise. Parade, September 9, 2001

Web Sites:

Original Complaint Filed in U.S. District Washington, D.C. www.indiantrust.com, June 10, 1996.

Not An "Other". www.onlinenewshour.com, July 16, 1997.

A Racial Tug of War Over Census. www.washingtonpost.com, March 3, 2000.

Interview with 60 Minutes. www.indiantrust.com, April 2, 2000.

This Land Is Not Your Land. www.courant.com, December 10, 2000.

Elouise Cobell Interview with Native America Calling. www.indiantrust.com, January 4, 2001.

Prediction for 2100: Twice the Americans. www.washingtonpost.com, January 13, 2000.

2000 Census Was Best Ever, Study Says, But Its Very Accuracy Spars Partisan Fighting Over Need for Statistical Adjustment. www.sacbeenews archive, February 15, 2001.

Census Broadens Race Category. www.thedesertsun.com, February 23, 2001.

Cobell v. Norton: An Overview. www.indiantrust.com, February 23, 2001.

Hispanics Draw Even With Blacks In New Census. www.washingtonpowysiwyg.com, March 7, 2001.

Census Shows Increasingly Diverse Nation. www.arizonare-public.com, March 9, 2001.

Census Finds Diversity Spreading to Suburbs. www.washingtonpost.com., March 9, 2001.

Mixed Feelings Over Multiracial Census Queries. www.sacbeenews archive, March 11, 2001.

Census 2000 Profile: American Indians in the United States. www.indiantrust.com, March 13, 2001.

Multiracial Growth Seen In Census. www.washingtonpost.com, March 13, 2001.

Census 2000 Blurs Black-or-White Issue. Some Fear Multiracial Snapshot Could Harm Civil Rights Efforts. www.jsonline.com, March 18, 2001.

Bibliography

The Changing Face of Metro Atlanta. www.accessatlanta.com, March 23, 2001.

11 States Show Fewer Whites in Latest Census. www.arizonarepublic.com, March 30, 2001.

California's Ethnic Diversity Grows. www.washingtonpost.com., March 30, 2001.

Racial Integration's Shifting Patterns. www.washingtonpost.com, April 1, 2001.

As Milwaukee's Population Diversifies, Metro Area Still Ranks Among Nation's Most Segregated. www.jsonline.com, April 3, 2001.

Mixed-Race Heritage, Mixed Emotions. www.washingtonpost.com, April 16, 2001.

Reversing a Long Pattern, Blacks Are Heading South. www.washingtonpost.com, May 5, 2001.

Shifting Portrait of U.S. Hispanics. www.washingtonpost.com, May 10, 2001.

Married-With-Children Still Fading. www.washingtonpost.com., May 15, 2001.

Two-Parent Families Increasingly Immigrants. www.washingtonpost.com., May 23, 2001.

Multiple Race Identities Most Common Among Children, Nonwhite Populations. www.mnplan.state.mn.us, May 29, 2001.

Amid New York's Sea of Faces, Islands of Segregation. www.nytimes.com, June 18, 2001.

1990s Further Reshape Suburbs. www.washingtonpost.com., June 25, 2001.

Scientists Debate Role of Race. www.yahoo.com, June 28, 2001.

Minority Ownership Still in Rise. www.chicagotribune.com, July 7, 2001.

Racial Identification Government: Color-blind? Or Blinded? The Irrelevance of Race. www.sfgate.com, July 8, 2001.

Making Sense of the New Census, Is America on the Verge of Transcending Race. www.sfgate.com, July 11, 2001.

Why I Checked Black on the Census. www.sfgate.com, July 11, 2001.

One Racial Barrier Is Disappearing. www.chicagotribune.com, July 12, 2001.

Why They Ask What They Ask. www.washingtonpost.com., July 16, 2001.

Are Interior and Treasury Corralled At Long Last? www.indiantrust.com, July 17, 2001.

At BIA, Seeking More For Tribes to Bet On. www.indiantrust.com, July 24, 2001.

Attempt to Limit Trust Fund Probe Rejected. www.indiantrust.com, July 24, 2001.

Government Criticized for Erasing E-mail Records in Indian Trust Fund Case. www.indiantrust.com, July 30, 2001.

Cobell Plaintiffs Ask Judge To Set Date For Trial On Trust Accounting. www.indiantrust.com, August 6, 2001.

Trust Fund Holders Want Trial Against Bush Officials. www.indiantrust.com, August 7, 2001.

Computer System Designed to Track Indian Money May Not Be Salvageable. www.indiantrust.com, August 9, 2001.

Babbitt Misled Judge About New System For Indian Trust Funds, Report Alleges. www.indiantrust.com, August 10, 2001.

Court Report Criticizes Trust Fund Software. www.indiantrust.com, August 10, 2001.

Judge Rejects Treasury Attempts To Keep Report On Document Destruction and Attorney Misconduct From The Public. www.indiantrust.com, August 14, 2001.

Light Punishment For Destroyed Trust Fund Records. www.indiantrust.com, August 15, 2001.

Discipline Records on Trusts Unsealed. www.indiantrust.com, August 15, 2001.

U.S. Agency Admits Errors in Indian Case; Records Destroyed on Cash Payouts. www.indiantrust.com, August 15, 2001.

Treasury Department Retrained Lawyers After Rubin Was Cited in Case, Papers Say. www.indiantrust.com, August 15, 2001.

Treasury Inquiry Finds No Wrongdoing in Destruction of Indian Affairs Documents. www.indiantrust.com, August 15, 2001.

No More Delays On Trust Fund. www.indiantrust.com, August 17, 2001.

Justice Plans Action For Destroyed Trust Records. www.indiantrust.com, August 17, 2001.

A Tale of Deceit, Abuse in D.C. Report: Interior Lied About System Tracking Indian Trust Accounts. www.indiantrust.com, August 19, 2001.

Where Did the Money Go? www.indiantrust.com, August 20, 2001.

300,000 Indians Cheated By Incompetent Feds. www.indiantrust.com, August 21, 2001.

Lawyer Urges Interior Misconduct Probe. www.indiantrust.com, August 22, 2001.

Peter Maas, Writer Who Chronicled the Mafia, Dies at 72. www.indiantrust.com, August 24, 2001.

Plaintiffs Press Judge to Hold Norton, Other Government Officials in Contempt. www.indiantrust.com, August 27, 2001.

Bibliography

Trust Fund Holders Call For Contempt. www.indiantrust.com, August 28, 2001.

Norton's 'Historic' Dump May Haunt Her. www.indiantrust.com, September 4, 2001.

Interior Delaying Trust Reform Report. www.indiantrust.com, September 7, 2001

Indian Trust Reform Still Mired, Watchdog Says Receivership Urged for Interior Program. www.indiantrust.com, September 8, 2001.

Cobell v. Babbitt: Case Chronology. www.indiantrust.com, September 10, 2001.

Cobell v. Norton: An Overview. www.indiantrust.com, September 10, 2001.

Few Dates Provided in Trust Fund Blueprint. www.indiantrust.com, September 13, 2001.

Court Monitor Finds BIA Trust Data Cleanup In "Disarray". www.indiantrust.com, September 17, 2001.

New Report Another Blow to Government Reform of Trust Fund for Indian Lands. www.indiantrust.com, September 18, 2001.

Interior Infighting Hampering Trust Fund Fix. www.indiantrust.com, September 20, 2001.

Norton Hit Over Tribal-Money Inaction. www.indiantrust.com, September 23, 2001.

Court-Appointed Investigator Recommends Judge Hold Norton in Contempt. www.indiantrust.com, October 1, 2001.

Norton Appears Closer to Citation for Contempt. www.indiantrust.com, October 2, 2001.

Trust Fund Fix At 'Great Risk' of Failure. www.indiantrust.com, October 10, 2001.

Memo: Solicitor's Order Was 'Intimidating'. www.indiantrust.com, October 10, 2001.

The Case of the Missing Report. www.indiantrust.com, October 10, 2001.

Trust Fund Progress 'Stretches Credibility'. www.indiantrust.com, October 11, 2001.

Norton Faulted on Indian Trusts. www.indiantrust.com, October 17, 2001.

Cobell v. Babbitt: Biography of Elouise Cobell. www.indiantrust.com, October 17, 2001.

Census Documents:

United States Census 2000

Overview of Race and Hispanic Origin. Census 2000 Brief, March 2001.

Mapping Census 2000: The Geography of U.S. Diversity. Census 2000 Special Reports.

Articles From The Carter G. Woodson Series:

Beasley, Delilah L.: Thomas Jefferson Thoughts On the Negro. The Journal of Negro History, Vol. III, No. 1, January 1918.

Woodson, Carter G.: The Relations of Negroes and Indians in Massachusetts. Vol. V, No. 1, January 1920.

Johnston, James Hugo: Documentary Evidence of the Relations of Negroes and Indians. Vol. XIV, No. 1, January 1929.

Porter Kenneth W.: Relations Between Negroes and Indians Within Limits of The United States. The Journal of Negro History, Vol. XVII, No. 3, July 1932.

Preston Jr. E.D.: Genesis of The Underground Railroad. Vol. XVIII, No. 2, April, 1933.

Winston, Sanford: Indian Slavery in the Carolina Region. The Journal of Negro History, Vol. XIX, No. 4, 1934.

Krugman, Marion Wilton: The Racial Composition of the Seminole Indians of Florida and Oklahoma, 1961.

Articles - The Journal of Negro History:

Graham, Pearl M.: Thomas Jefferson and Sally Hemings. Vol. XLVI, No. 2, April 1961.

McCloy, Shelby T.: Negroes and Mulattoes In Eighteenth Century France. Vol. XXX, No. 2, July 1945.

Porter, Kenneth W.: Florida Slaves and Free Negroes In The Seminole War, 1835-1842. Vol. XXVIII, No. 4, October 1943.

Smith, Lynn. The Redistribution of The Negro Population of The United States 1910-1960. Vol. 1, No. 3, July 1966.

Census Chronology:

1790
The nation's first census 650 federal marshals go house-to-house unannounced, writing down the name of the head of the household and counting the other residents. The census costs $45,000, takes 18 months and counts 3.9 million people.

1810
First inquiries on U.S. manufacturing capabilities are made. At the time, the need to export agricultural products and import manufactured goods had entangled the U.S. in some skirmishes of the Napoleonic Wars.

1840
Congress requests new information on social matters such as "idiocy" and mental illness. Many questions on commerce and industry are added, lengthening the form to 80 questions.

Bibliography

1850
Significant census reforms are made. Federal government marshals scientific and financial resources to discuss what should be asked, how the information should be collected and how it should be reported. First time detailed information about all members of a household is collected.

1860
Data from the 1860 Census is used during the Civil War to measure relative military strengths and manufacturing abilities of the Union and Confederacy.

1890
Major innovations are made to the "science of statistics" as the Census Bureau introduces mechanical tabulators. Never again is the census hand tabulated.

1910
Entry into World War I (1917) has agencies and policymakers turning to the Census Bureau for industrial statistics to plan the war effort.

1930
The onset of the Great Depression prompts the Census Bureau to make inquiries about unemployment, migration and income.

1940
With the aid of modern sampling techniques, the Census Bureau creates the first "long form" that is sent to only a subset of the population.

1950
First electronic digital computer tabulates figures 1,000 to 1 million times faster than previous equipment.

1970
People of Hispanic or Spanish descent asked to identify themselves as such.

1980
After the 1980 count, the Census Bureau faces 54 lawsuits, many by civil rights groups, charging it with improper and unconstitutional methods of counting.

2000
First time professional advertising campaign ($167 million) is used to promote the count.

www.washingtonpost.com, July 16, 2001.

Photo Credits

U.S. Signal Corps. Archives	2	Chicago Historical Society	66
U.S. Signal Corps. Archives	4	Chicago Tribune	67
U.S. Signal Corps. Archives	4	Negro Yearbook	68
U.S. Signal Corps Archives	5	Lloyd G. Wheeler	70
U.S. Signal Corps. Archives	6	Urban Research Press	71
U.S. Signal Corps. Archives	7	U.S. Signal Corps	72
U.S. Signal Corps. Archives	8	Urban Research Press	75
U.S. Signal Corps. Archives	9	Associated Press	78
Maryland Historical Society	11	U.S. Signal Corps	83
U.S. Archives	12	U.S. Signal Corps	84
U.S. Archives	14	U.S. History Archives	85
U.S. Archives	17	U.S. History Archives	86
U.S. Archives	18	U.S. History Archives	87
Urban Research Press	21	U.S. History Archives	88
Urban Research Press	22	U.S. History Archives	89
Urban Research Press	23	U.S. History Archives	90
Urban Research Press	24	U.S. Signal Corps	91
Urban Research Press	26	U.S. Signal Corps	92
Urban Research Press	29	Urban Research Press	93
Urban Research Press	32	U.S. History Archives	94
Urban Research Press	33	U.S. History Archives	96
Urban Research Press	38	Associated Press	97
Urban Research Press	40		
Urban Research Press	41		
Urban Research Press	42		
Urban Research Press	45		
Urban Research Press	47		
Urban Research Press	50		
Urban Research Press	51		
Chicago Defender	52		
Negro Yearbook	56		
Lloyd G. Wheeler	60		
U.S. Archives	62		
Negro Yearbook	64		
Lloyd G. Wheeler	65		

Index

Index

Index